GEORGIA, ALABAMA AND SOUTH CAROLINA PAPERS

GEORGIA ALABAMA AND SOUTH CAROLINA PAPERS

Volume 1V of the Draper Manuscript Collection

Transcribed and Indexed by
Craig L. Heath

HERITAGE BOOKS
2006

HERITAGE BOOKS
AN IMPRINT OF HERITAGE BOOKS, INC.

Books, CDs, and more—Worldwide

For our listing of thousands of titles see our website
at
www.HeritageBooks.com

Published 2006 by
HERITAGE BOOKS, INC.
Publishing Division
65 East Main Street
Westminster, Maryland 21157-5026

International Standard Book Number: 978-0-7884-3562-0

INTRODUCTION

This volume of the *Draper Manuscripts* is concerned in large part with the military career of Gen. Elijah Clarke of Georgia, and with his son, John Clarke, Governor of Georgia; with Maj. Benjamin Few, Col. William Candler, Col. Micajah Williamson, and other participants in the conflicts in Georgia during and after the Revolutionary War; with the early history of Moravian missions in Georgia, Pennsylvania, and Ohio; with the lives and adventures of Alexander McGilvery, David Tate, and William Weatherford in Alabama during the period of the War of 1812; with an account of the Creek Indians written by George Stiggins; and with miscellaneous papers relating to the Yazoo Land Company in South Carolina.

This transcription of the *Georgia, Alabama and South Carolina Papers* was made from the 1980 microfilm edition of the *Draper Manuscripts, Volume IV*. Large portions of some documents in this volume are illegible or poorly legible, mainly owing to fading. Where illegible, these portions (whether single words or entire passages) are indicated by ellipses (…); some effort has been made to interpret poorly legible portions, but the original manuscript or microfilm copy should be consulted for verification. The transcript should be viewed as an aid to use of the manuscript, rather than a replacement or substitute for it, and users are urged to consult the original manuscript or the microfilm in parallel with the transcript.

Document numbers/page numbers are stamped on the pages of the original manuscript. These are indicated in brackets at the beginning of each page in the transcript. In many cases, the beginning page of a document has a cardinal number as page number (e.g. [p. 66]), and subsequent pages in the same document have the same cardinal number with a superscript (e.g. [p. 66^{1}], [p. 66^{2}], etc.). Owing to the variability in length of text on the manuscript pages, no attempt has been made to correlate page breaks in the transcript with those in the manuscript.

The spelling, punctuation, capitalization, and grammar used in the original documents have been preserved so far as feasible. Dashes have generally been replaced with appropriate punctuation. In some cases, a word or phrase at the end of a line or page was repeated at the beginning of the next line or page of the original document; these repetitions are reproduced in the transcription.

In the Table of Contents, fuller descriptions of some of the documents are appended in small typeface after the title or main description, for the user's convenience.

The Draper Manuscript Collection is owned by the Wisconsin Historical Society, Madison, Wisconsin. The cooperation of the society in the production of this volume is hereby gratefully acknowledged.

TABLE OF CONTENTS

(Letters are addressed to Lyman C. Draper unless otherwise noted.)

VOLUME 1V
GEORGIA, ALABAMA, AND SOUTH CAROLINA PAPERS

Georgia.
Elijah Clarke.
Wm. Candler.

[p. 1]
Memos. about Gen. Elijah Clarke, of Georgia.

Sherwood's Gazetteer, of Georgia states that Clarke was born in Rutherford Co., N. C. "about 1749". I infer he was born several years earlier, for two reasons:

1st. His widow, Hannah Clarke, died, Aug. 1827, aged 90, which would fix her birth year 1737: and it is not probable she was a dozen years older than her husband.

2d. If Gen. Clark was born abt. 1749, his son John who figured first as a Lieut. then a Captain, under his father, in the Revolution, serving as a Captain in 1780, & probably a Lieut in 1779, say at sixteen, would show that
16
he was born about 1763, when Gen. Clark, his father, if born abt. 1749, was only fourteen.

White's Histl. Collns. Georgia, p. 229, says John Clarke was appd. a Lieut. at sixteen. Drake's Biographical Dictionary repeats this, saying he was born in 1766, which, if correct, would make him, when serving as Captain in 1780, only 14 years old, a palpable error. White's Georgia, as above, says John Clark died in Octr., 1832, in his 67th year, wh. wd. fix his birth in 1766. He must have been 3 or

4 years older.

[p. 1[1]]

In 1750, Col. Clark emigrated from Virginia & settled on Pacolet river

Ramsey's Hist. S. C. i, p. 207,208.

Col. Edwd. Clark's letter, shows Gen Elijah Clark was 57 when he died in Dec. 1799, which would indicate 1742 as his birth year, which is no doubt correct.

1780, June, Clark joins Sumter =

Dr. John Winsmith's statement,
Maj. Smith's pension papers.
Johnson's Traditions, 341.

Sherwood's Georgia Gazetteer says Gen E. Clarke settled near Mallarysville, Wilkes Co, which is the northern part of the county as shown by the map in White's Histl. Collns.; & a memoir of the General's widow in the same volume, p. 682, says she was buried at Wooburn, near the remains of her husband.

[p. 1a]

Col. Elijah Clarke, 1780.

"Charleston, Nov. 26, 1780.

On the 14th of September last, a party of Americans under the command of Lieut. Col. Clarke, of the militia of Georgia, crossed the river Savannah, about sixty miles above Augusta, made a rapid march down to that town, and attacked the detachment of the British army stationed there, under the command of Lieut. Col. Brown, killed and wounded a great many of the regular troops, and about seventy of the Indians. The whole of the British troops must inevitably have fallen into the hands of the Americans, had not a re-inforcement arrived from Ninety Six, a station in South Carolina, about fifty miles distant from Augusta, which obliged Col. Clarke to retreat; which he did with the loss of about twenty three men killed and wounded; but not without carrying off a great supply of ammunition, and the greatest part of the goods deposited there as presents for the Indians. After Clarke's retreat some few prisoners were taken; eleven of whom were hanged on the spot, without even the formality of a trial; some were given up to the savage barbarity of the Indians, who were first scalped, and afterwards put to death. Shuddering humanity recoils on itself, and the cheek of honor redden-

[p. 1a[1]]

eth with indignation at the recital. While this tragedy was acting, I kept close at home, not thinking it prudent even to be a spectator on the occasion."

"Savannah, in Georgia, Oct. 5. We hear from Augusta, that thirteen men have been lately hanged there, for having joined Clarke in his attack on Col. Brown, after taking the oaths of allegiance to the British government."

"New York, Nov. 29. The enterprise of the rebels against Augusta miscarried, through the firmness of Col. Brown, supported through the opportune arrival of Col. Cruger, on which occasion the rebels ran away. Col. Cruger found a rascal among the rebel prisoners, one Dukes, who after having submitted to government, and taken the oaths, was found in arms at Augusta, whom he ordered to be hanged."

Scots Magazine, Jan. 1781, pp. 22, 23.

[p. 1b]

Col. Elijah Clarke, of Georgia, 1780.

Col. Clarke, with one hundred riflemen, forced his way through South Carolina to Georgia; and, on his route thither, being joined by seven hundred men, he proceeded to the town of Augusta and took it [only attacked it. L. C. D.]; but not finding it prudent to continue there, he retreated to the upper part of South Carolina in Ninety Six District, and made a stand with eight hundred men.

Histl. Jourl. of Revn. in 1st series, Vol. 2d Mass. Hist Colls.

[Maj. Dunlap's Defeat] Dec. 16, 1780, Col. Tarleton's Legion received a severe repulse in attempting to surprise Colonels Marion and Clarke, who with a detachment of five or six hundred men, were posted in the District of Ninety Six. Upwards of a hundred of the enemy were left dead on the Spot, and a great Number wounded. Tarleton [...or] having received many wounds, returned to Charleston. By the account given of this affair, the loss of the Continentals did not exceed ten in killed and wounded.

Historical Journal, as above

[p. 1b[1]]

In Callender's "Annual Register for 1796", p. 84, reference is made to Gen. Clark's independent effort of 1794.

Chappell's Georgia's "Miscellanies" gives the fullest estimate of Clark's acts of 1794, I have noticed.

[p. 1c]

May the 19th 1782.

Sir, as I was on my way down with a party of men there Came interligance after me of my family being killed by the Indians and some Others which Caused me to Return back there will be a Number of men at agustea very Shotly on their way to join Genl. Wane which I hope youl forward on I beg youl Excuse Shortness of my Letter as I am in Great hast

From Sir your most H Obdt
Elijah Clark

[p. 1c[1]]
Colo. Elijah Clark
19 May 1782
Military

To
The Honourable
John Martin Esqr
Governour of the
State of Georgia

[p. 1d]
Der. Sir/ Watorsfort May 29th 1782

I have Recievd yours of 23d and 27th & am much oblige to you for the Arly Intiligeance. Every precaution in my power Shall be taken to prevent the British hirlings from Executing their Cruel and Bloody Designs on the good Citizens of the State. Since my Last to you there Came in a party of Indians atacked a block house on the Twenty third aftor keeping up a fire for Some time they went of killing Six head of Cattle and every valuable horse they ware persued by Capt Barber to the South fork of the oaconcy which must be nere whare Mctask is to Rondyvoue but his horses failing he wass obliged to Return. on the Twenty fifth an other party of about fiften Indians appered neare a Station in the fork of Brod River & Savanah where the Shot and kiled a mn, those which the Scalpd. & appered as if the ment to Storm but by the Spireted Exartion of four men onley that wass at the Station Saling out Put the Invaidors to Such a Surprise [p. 1d[1]]

They went of in grate presapitation Major dooly having a Party of Collected on the first occation march'd Before Day to whare they murder wass Done persued two Days but for want of horses Sufficient to folow on he wass forced to Return they Indians not striking Camp the hole way the major went Though Capt barber on his Return Fell in with Them had a scanmage Drove the Indians took all thair Budgets and provision Retook the Scalps they maid thair Escape by Taking to Large Cain swamp the Last mischife Done onley five miles from whare I Live. I Send orders for Colos. Martin & Lee to meet me at the Place of Rondey-vous if I Can have a few Days to Collect the Molitia & McIntosh Meets at the peech tree & we Can fall in with his party I hope we Shall be able to give a good Account of them

Ples to Inform General wayn the Resons of my not going Dow to Camp by the first oppertunity) by the Conduct of the British Amissaries & Savages they appere as if they Intended to Disappoint us in our planting Buisines and prevent us from Securing our Small grain as they have maid frequent Inrods on our Settlements in a Short time.

I am with grate Respect and Estem E. Clark

Governor Martin

[p. 1e]

Dear Sir

I came here yesterday being informed that Mr. Maiker is going your way & embraced the opportunity to inform you that I recd. £18 from Jackson for you £15 of which is Morises note which will be Due the first of march & will endevour to get it Changed for you by the time you are ... Please to present my Best Compts. to Mrs. Clark & belive me to be with much Esteem

Dr. Sir yours &c
John MacDonald

Long medows }
Feby. 14th 1783 }

To Col Elijah Clarke
Col Clark

Doctor McDonald
Feb. 14, 1783

[p. 1f]

Georgia Augusta 9th Decr. 1794.

Dr. Sir

I have impatiently Waited an answer to my letters which I have repeatedly wrote you but invain. I thought however I should have heard from you by Major Arrington or Colo. Dooly. But every expectation being dissappointed I embrace this opportunity with pleasure to inform you what our Assembly are about. In consequence of Several Petitions from different Companies, the Committee to whom they were referred have reported favourably and to this effect respecting the Vacant Territory of this State. That the State of Georgia is recognised by the various Treaties with Foreign Nations a free And Independant State &c. The reserves for the accomodation of her Citizens all that tract of Vacant territory extending as far as the Chattahouchi, And proposeth selling the Ballance to the Westerd & Southerd to the Applicants agreeable to their offer &c. ther is the Substance of the report which now lies before the House for debate. I have not a doubt but the Bill will pass both Houses but some are of opinion that the Governor will negative it. This is the only business of Consequence which hath, or I believe will come before the Assembly this Session.

I understand that your Legislative body are now

sitting, and have it in Contemplation to open a land office: Should this be the Case there will thousands

[p. 1f[1]]

flock from this Country to Kentucky for these reasons first there are Numbers of inhabitants here who could go to your State, but their finances are at such a low ebb, they cannot purchase those lands already located. the Scond reason is the Sicklyness of this Country: There never has been as many people Sick Since I came to this State in the back Country as have last season if they ware all added together, which circumstance hath disgusted the Inhabitants generally healthy before, to Such a degree that they would rather live a Hunters life in the bleak Mountains than Continue where they are.

I beg you will give me a description of your State, of the advantages and disadvantages which would naturally Accrue to a new Settler. I am disgusted with this State and intend to visit yours in the Spring, but previous to my arrival, should wish to have the best information respecting the Country which I can collect, respecting the most eligable mode of settling and the best part of the Country to settle in, together with every other information which you may think people to give.

Colo. Dannel moved to Kentucky from this State by whom I promised to write you. I had not an opportunity at the time he set off but I can assure you that he is a Gentleman who was highly esteemed in this State by all who knew him, and I hope should you get acquainted with him, you will pay him

[p. 1f[2]]

all the attention which a letter of recommendation from me could possibly merit. This will be handed to you by Mr.

Dickinson attorney at law, a gentleman whom I recommend to your particular attention. he has gone to transact Some business in your State, and every Curtesy to him from you will add to the many Obligations already conferred on

Dr. Sir Your Sincere friend & Hul. Servt.

Elijah Clarke

See Drakes Biog Dict. Am. No. 22

Gen. Elijah Clarke. Born in N. C. Removed to Geo in 1774. Capt in 1776. Subsequently Brig Genl of ... he defeated the British at Musgroves Mill & Blackstocks & contributed greatly to the Capture of Augusta in June 1781. Severely Wounded; aftds. joined the Command of Genl. Pickens. He afterward fought many battles & made Several treaties with the Creek Indians. He died in Wilkes Co. Geo. Dec 15, 1799 (next day after Washington died.)

Drakes Am "Biog Dict."

Genl. E Clarke
Hond. p }
Mr. Dickenson }

Governor Shelby.
Kentucky

No. 88

[p. 1g]
342

Revolutionary Genl. Elijah Clarke

Captn. then Brig. Genl. of Georgia troops in the Amn. Revy. War. Defeated the British at Musgrove's Mill and Blackstock's, & was Severely Wounded. Served afterwards under Genl. Pickens in S. C. Fought many battles & made several treaties with the Creek Indians. Died Dec 15, 1799.

See Drake's Biogl. Dicty.

A Lt. 2½ pp 4to Augusta Geo. 1794.
To Governor Isaac Shelby of Ky.

[p. 1g[1]]
Excerpt from "Daughters of the American Revolution Magazine", August 1916, p. 126.

4532. CLARKE. Elijah Clarke was born in Edgecombe Co. N. C. in 1733; m Hannah Arrington in N. C. in 1762; moved to Wilkes Co. Ga. between 1774 and 1777. He was never Gov. of Ga. It was his son, John Clarke who was Governor (1818-1820). The children of Elijah according to Mr. Josiah H. Shinn, 624 Rock Creek Church Road, Washington, D. C. were: Elijah, b 1764 m Miss Long; Gov. John, b Edgecombe Co. N. C. Feb. 28, 1766, d Oct. 12, 1832 m in Ga. Nancy Williamson and had four children; and two daughters. According to Miss Frances Mounger (who unfortunately does not give her address), there were: Sarah, who m Josiah Walton of Wilkes Co.; Elizabeth, who m Benajah Smith; Nancy, who m Jesse Thompson of Elbert Co.; Polly (Mary) who m Charles Williamson (of Wilkes Co. Ga.). He lived only two years and she m (2) Wm. I. Hobby of Augusta; Susan who d in childhood; Fannie a twin of Elijah (who m Margaret Long of Wilkes Co.) who m Edwin Mounger of Wilkes Co. and Gibson, who d unmarried.

[p. 2]

Augusta Ga.
... 15th 1871

My ...

I am ...ved two days ago ... you are engaged on such a work & it will give me pleasure to give you all the information I can obtain about my great grandfather, Gen

Elijah Clarke. As soon as I can collect my information I will forward it. I will ...

I write now only ... the ... & that I will ... the Pamphlets ... for the ...

From ... Sevt.
Jos. McWhorter

... addressed me as ... Joseph McWhorter, that ...

[p. 3]

Augusta Georgia,
March 1st 1872.

Lyman C. Draper Esqr:
Madison, Wis:

My Dear Sir,

I regret very much that I have been so much delayed in furnishing you with information about Gen: Elijah Clarke, of Georgia, & I regret still more that, what I now furnish you is so meager.

I had hoped to procure for you a large amount of valuable, original historical matter from my cousin Mrs. Ann Campbell, a daughter of Gov. John Clarke. But unfortunately all the papers & documents in her possession, containing many original letters of Gen. Elijah Clarke, were destroyed by fire in 1845, as you will see by a copy of her letter herewith inclosed. Judge Campbell said they were worth their weight in diamonds. They would, undoubtedly,

[p. 3[1]]
have thrown a great deal of light upon the history of those times. You cannot imagine my disappointment at this loss.

I inclose you some copies of letters received from Judge Campbell, Mrs. Ann Campbell & Mrs. Hobson, grand daughters of Gen. Elijah Clarke, from which you can select what you wish.

I also inclose an obituary written by the late Gen. James Jackson, the original being in the possession of the Historical Society of this Sate.

For other information I can only refer you now, to McCall's history "Whites Statistics of Georgia" & "Whites Historical Collections of Georgia" & the life of Gen: Greene.

I am now trying to get a photograft of the portrait of Gen: Clarke in the possession of Mrs. Pickens. As soon as I can get it I will send it to you.

If there is any thing I can do for you in this part of the

[p. 3[2]]

country by way of furthering your purposes, I will be very glad to assist you. If you think of any thing please let me know.

I inclose, also, a condensed statement of information written by my wife, who has taken some interest in looking up the history of Gen. Clarke.

I will take very great pleasure in reading your book when it is published, & look forward to it with some impatience.

Please acknowledge the receipt of these papers.

I am, very Respectfully,
Your Obt. Servant,
Geo. G. McWhorter

Col: Williamson was the Grandfather of Judge John A. Campbell who can tell you all you wish to know about him. Wilson Lumpkin is dead. I do not propose to publish any thing myself, about Gen: Clarke.

[p. 4]

Remarks by Mrs. McWhorter.

From all the data to be obtained it is very clear that Gen. Elijah Clarke was a very prominent, efficient & distinguished officer during the Revolution, & afterwards in suppressing the Indians, who kept up a continued & annoying warfare against the frontier, for years after the separation from Great Britain. Of his career during the Revolution information may be obtained from McCall. Though, as Judge Campbell states, McCall was influenced by party feeling, & did not do him justice. Certain it is that as commander of a regiment of Georgia Troops, he alone withstood the British arms when South Carolina & the rest of Georgia had been forced to yield temporary submission. In the upper part of Georgia, Clarke was the only bulwark against the British. After the failure of his attempt to take Augusta, he gathered the distressed handfull of disappointed veterans, women & children, with such effects as

[p. 4[1]]

they could carry, & conducted the dejected caravan through Tennessee & into Kentucky. Placing the women & children in places of safety, he & what remained of his regiment, joined the army that was marching from North Carolina through South Carolina & was thus again in the field. After the fall of Savannah his principle operations were against the Indians. These he, in a measure kept in check, though he complained of insufficient support from the General Government.

Of his difficulties with the General Government there are no records in the family. They certainly arose from the repudiation on the part of the Government of the treaties Clarke & others had made with the Indians from time to time, acting for the State, & these treaties were accepted by the State. Clarke was acquitted by a jury in his own County when he was tried, & the General Government afterwards gave Georgia the right to control matters in her own Territories,

[p. 4[2]]
which showed that, although Gen. Clarke may have acted too much on his own responsibility in resisting the action of the General Government, still his position was not unjustifiable, though perhaps unwise. He was certainly a great military genius, & his reputation must have been extended when England & France should both have been anxious to engage him in their services, & they each offered him great inducements. There are very complimentary accounts of him in "Whites Historical Collections of Georgia" & "Whites Statistics of Georgia."

It is only another evidence of the fickleness of public opinion, & also of its ingratitude when the memory of a prominent man like Gen: Clarke, & one on whom all relied in times of trial & danger, should be suffered to drop into oblivion, merely because other parties sprang up of opposing politics, & party rancor was so great that every one who differed in opinion was traduced. So goes the world.

[p. 4[3]]
The loss of the letters & papers of which Mrs. Campbell writes cannot be too much regretted, as they would, undoubtedly, have thown a great deal of light on the History of the times. That Gen. Clarke should have taken matters in his own hands a good deal is not surprising, when it is remembered that to him was confided, principally the defence of the frontier against the Indians, whose attacks were so sudden that, no time was allowed for consultation

either with the State, or General Government. Those in command were necessarily obliged to be a law unto themselves in those days of disorder & chaos.

Gen. Clarke & those fighting with him may certainly be excused for feeling a considerable degree of irritation against the General Government, & may, also, be excused, to a great extent, for the resistance they made to the action taken by the Government in the matters of the treaties, when it is remembered that, after the

[p. 4[4]]

trials, difficulties, hardships & dangers they underwent in the harrassing warfare with the Indians, and after the Indians had been brought fairly & honorably to sign important treaties from time to time, that the Government should, without consultation with the State authorities, have sent a secret embassy to Gen. Pickens (who was not a citizen of the State of Georgia) & by his assistance have enticed McGillavry & other of the Indian Chiefs to New York, & there have arranged with them that they should retain certain lands that had already been ceded to the State of Georgia, & which were then under cultivation by Citizens of the State.

The State certainly appreciated his services, for she gave him a large & valuable plantation, situated on the Savannah river, near Petersburg, which was, at that time, a flourishing town in Georgia, in grateful acknowledgement for what he had done for the

[p. 4[5]]

State in the times that tried men's souls. He bore many honorable Scars which spoke for themselves, & was long remembered admiringly & affectionately in the State. Up to the time of his death he was almost continuously in the field, for the Indians were incessant in their attacks.

Gen: Elijah Clarke died in 1799 & as late as '93 we find him exerting a controlling influence in a council convened by Gov: Telfair to determine as to the defences of the frontier, the General Government having been applied to, in vain, for assistance. His Son, Gen: John Clarke (afterwards Governor) was intrusted with the defence of the Sea Coast & Southern boundary of Georgia, in the war of 1812.

Mrs. Geo. G. McWhorter

January 1872

[p. 5]
... jah ... jah ...

[p. 5^1]
heart by John Clark's ... daughter ... I have ... men. I should be glad ...

[p. 5^2]
... Mrs McTunquimy ... I do wish ... ...jah

[p. 5^3]
... for so ... I ... always ...

[p. 6]

Augusta Ga.
April 22d 1872.

Lyman C. Draper Esqire
Madison, Wis.

Dear Sir,

On the receipt of your last letter I wrote to a friend in Raleigh N. C. for information about Gen: Elijah Clarke's family & that of his wife, who was Miss Arrington. He promised to do what he could in the premises. I also wrote to Wilkes County to get the inscription on the tombstone of Gen: Clarke & his wife, & should have had it by this time. When I get the above information will forward it immediately.

John Clarke was a mere youth when he commanded a Company under his father at the siege of Augusta; I think only fifteen.

Charles C. Jones, formerly of Savannah Ga., now of New York City, has recently obtained a book

[p. 6[1]]

written by T. N. P. Charton, from London, Eng. It is a history ..., who wrote the obituary of Gen: Clarke, which I sent you. It no doubt contains much information about Clarke. ...vannah ... of Revolutionary times, (I forget the title) that Jones told me contained information of Gen: Clarke. As you have had some correspondence with him, ...fore ... he can, no doubt, give you further information about these ... If I can get the Photograft of Gen. Clarke I will ... it to you ...

Very Respectfully, Yours &c
Geo. G. McWhorter

[p. 7]

Augusta Ga
Jany 4th 1873.

Lyman C. Draper Esqr
Dear Sir,

I would have answered you much sooner than this but have been endeavoring to obtain the information you wished, both from the gravestones & from North Carolina. I have been entirely unsuccessful in both. A Gentleman living in the neighborhood of the old burying ground visited it to get the inscriptions for me & found every thing destroyed, except the inscription on the stone

[p. 7[1]]
of one of his daughters, my Grandmother.

There is nothing to mark the grave of Old Gen: Clarke now but a crumbled stone wall. I think it probable that the stones have been carried away at some time, & the whole place allowed to go to decay & ruin, the fate of all private burying grounds.

I have had several letters from North Carolina, but all to no purpose, I could get no light.

I shall not "weary in well doing" but get you all the information I can find. I will enquire further about the grave stones, in hope that

[p. 7[2]]
"something may turn up".

I thank you, very much, for the Vol. of Wisconsin Historical Collections you sent me.

They are very interesting documents, & will be very valuable to those who shall come after us.

I hope to be able to give you more information.

Very Respectfully,

Geo. G. McWhorter

[p. 8]

Augusta, Ga:
Oct. 11th 1873.

Lyman C Draper Esqr.
Madison, Wis:

Dear Sir,

Yours of the 13th Sept is received. For information about the Life of Jackson by Charlton I refer you to the

State Historical Society of Georgia, at Savannah, & to Gen: Henry R. Jackson of Savannah, & to Col: Charles C. Jones, now of New York City. They can give you information. A son of the late Gov: Hammond of S. C. has made diligent search among his fathers papers for the oration of Dr. J. McCad & can find nothing relating to it. He found a letter written by Gen: Sumter on nullification matters which he promised to copy & give me. I will send it to you. For information write to Thomas Sumter, Stateburg, S. C. & to Prof. Maximilian Laborde, Columbia S. C. & to Isaac Hayne, of S. C. Cannot give you his particular address.

[p. 8[1]]

Dr. I. P. Garvin of this City, is a discondant of the Fews. He told me yesterday that Col: Benj. N. Few moved to Alabama & died in the Western part of the State on the waters of the Black Warrior, or Tombigbee. Write to him. Write particularly, to Mrs. Frances Chrystie, care of Wm. F. Chrystie Esqr, Hastings-on-Hudson, Westchester County, N. Y. Mrs. Chrystie is the daughter of Wm. Few, a brother of Benj. N. Few, & can no doubt give you much information, as she is a very bright & intelligent old lady now about 80 years old.

I would have answered your letter sooner but have been trying to get information for you. I will be glad to assist you in any way I can. I have failed so far in getting a photograph of old Gen Elijah Clarke, but if I can get one will send it. You may command me as far as I can assist you. Very Truly Yours &c.

Geo. G. McWhorter

[p. 9]

Augusta, Ga:
May 16th 1878.

Lyman C. Draper Esqr
Madison;
Dear Sir,

I have received yours of the 10th inst, & went to see Dr. Garvin, who told me that, he intended to reply to you, but has been prevented by an unusual amount of sickness in his family for the past three months, having had six cases of typhoid fever in it. Mrs. Caroline S. Thomas & her sister know nothing whatever about their Grandfather Benjn. Few, they never saw him, as he died long before they were born & their own father (son of B. F.) left them when they were small children & they never saw him afterwards, & they have no records of any kind. Maj. Benj. Few (as Dr. Garvin tells me) left here, & probably died, before 1803. He tried to get

[p. 9[1]]
his niece, Dr. Garvin's mother, to go with him, offering to give her all he had. She did not go with him & married in 1803, after Maj. Few had left. Maj. Few went to Alabama where he had a large quantity of land & settled in or about Claiborne, in Monroe County, Ala., & no one here knows when or where he died. I would suggest to you to write to the Clerk of the Court, of Monroe Co: to examine the records as to transfers of land; & also to the Ordinary or Surrogate of the Probate Court, where, perhaps, a will might be found. I do not know, now, how they style their courts in Alabama. You might in this way get some information, tho' the chance is slim. I think it probable that, his son the father of Caroline S. Thomas, when he left his family here, went to Monroe County. He married again & reared other children of whom Mrs.

[p. 9^{2}]
Thomas knows nothing.

I also went to see another Mrs. Thomas, a descendant of the Fews whose daughter married Wm. F. Chrystie of N. Y. & she could give me no information whatever. But very few records were kept in those days in this latitude & very few of what were kept have been preserved. The country was very sparsely settled by white people & Indians abounded on all sides, & all hostile, & families would have to move five or six times, or oftener, in the 12 months. In this way all old records, files, letters & papers were lost. I think Mrs. Campbell is not mistaken about her fathers age. Gov: John Clarke commanded a Company under his father, at the age of 14, & was at this place with his company when Gen: E. Clarke captured it from the British in 1780, or '81. (See McCalls Hist. Of Georgia). John Clarke died & is burried, at St. Andrews Bay, Fla:

[p. 9^{3}]
& a friend of mine, during the war told me he read the inscription on his tomb. Write to Post Master, or some other, at that place & get a copy of the inscription. I tried to get a copy of the inscription on the tomb of old Gen: Elijah Clarke but some one had stolen the slab, & it, no doubt, now adorns the back log in some negro's hut.

Will be pleased to assist you at any time if I can. Have you ever seen a book written by Absolom H. Chappel, of Macon or Columbus, Ga: called "Reminiscences" or "Recollections" of Ga:" in which he has a great deal to say about men of the times of General & Gov: Clarke. The book was written & published about two years ago. Chappell is a very old man, if not dead, & knew John Clarke & his cotemporaries.

Very Respectfully yours &c.
Geo. G. McWhorter

[p. 10]

Greensboro Ala. Oct. 17th ...

... McWhorter,

... John Clarke ... I knew ... has ... when I ... General ...

[p. 10^{2}]
... defense and British ... family ... Clark ... and Showed it ...

[p. 10^{3}]
... this task's ... could ... and ... had ... the ... to oppose ...

[p. 10^{4}]
... would get ...day when She was going ... her Saddle to carry it ... getting it from ... it to them, when they ... it up. She ... and try ... My uncle ...

[p. 10^{5}]
... I had ... comparing ...

[p. 10^{6}]
... family ...

[p. 10^{7}]
... I suppose he ... and ...

[p. 10^{8}]
... about ... Elijah and ... Clarke

[p. 11]

Prarie View June 3d/72

Mr. Geo. G. McWhorter

... call ... the only survivors ... has awakened ... both head ... You ask the particulars of ... Gen Elijah ... all ... it. The let... members ... tribute ... hearing and ...

[p. 11[1]]

... had charge ... and ... ... Clarke,

[p. 11[2]]

in this ... John's brother Elijah ... hope that ... Nearly ... Clark ... having ...Since ... name ... letters ... self having ... the ... ... John Clark ...

[p. 11[3]]

Draper ... before ... and ... Gen Elijah ... of the letters ...

[p. 11[4]]

... the 15th inst 1794 ... held ... him ... he was ...

[p. 11[5]]

might ... have ... the day ... Triggs ... act, ... Sumpter ... Triggs ... South Carolina ...

[p. 11[6]]

... General Wayne before ... to See ... relieves ... frightsome ... who rule by ... There ... to advance ... incurred ... of the ... thing the ... which he ...

[p. 11[7]]

during the revolutionary war has thought it his duty to Clarke and his family to give this little Sketch of his character, and although he always ... proved of his ... in foreign Service ... Florida yet ... Sold to assist the ... Clarke have ... that the ... Hero ...

General Clarke ... and I will in a ... and determined enemy ... an affectionate Parent.

... the ... impeachment ... of Rep... largely ...

This is a ... Jackson has ... Thomas Jackson now in my possession.

Joseph W. Jackson

[p. 12]

I do not know of any one who can aid you. Within the last few years all those I know of who had information have died.

Very Respectfully
J. A. Campbell

New Orleans
Jany 28 1871.

Lyman Draper Esq
Madison, Wis
Sir

Your letter of the 23rd Inst has been recd. I regret to inform you, that Mrs. Campbell the grand daughter of Genl Elijah Clarke, & daughter of Gov John Clark of Georgia some years ago informed me that the papers of her father and grandfather had been lost or destroyed in the changes of domical of the family.

She spoke of having had quite a volume of correspondence between Gov Clarke & the Spanish authorities of

[p. 12[1]]

Florida & Louisiana in which they proposed a separation of Georgia fm connection with the other states & their Union with the Spanish dominion shortly after the Revolutionary war. But no information could be had of the particulars of the Correspondence. From what I heard in early life of Genl. Clarke he must have been a ... character. He resided in Wilkes County Geo. near the Indian frontier. The tories from Carolina & Georgia found refuge among the Indians and fitted out expeditions of invasion from thence upon the white settlements. Their inroads were murderous & desolating. Nothing was spared whether

[p. 12^{2}]
of life or property.

Gen Clark commanded the regiment formed in Upper Georgia. My Grand father Williamson was the Lieut Col of that regiment & the son of the one, in each case married the daughter of the other after the war.

My maternal ancestor & her daughters passed through the war. I have heard them speak of Gen Clark. His determination & courage never quaverd. He was either victorious or, personally disabled in every battle.

The confidence he inspired was universal.

The inhabitants of that region reposed upon their opinion that he was

[p. 12^{3}]
always ready for service.

There has never been any proper reation of Gen Clark. An inveterate personal quarrel between Gov. Clark & Mr Crawford afterwards ending in a party division of bitterness & violence in Georgia has occasioned jaundiced views of all that related to the early history of the state.

The men of the revolution were depreciated & disperaged by the immigrants to the State after the war & great services in the calamity of the coloney have not been acknowledged but the acknowledgement would affect some party issue, then existing between their positions.

[p. 13]

New Orleans
28 N. 1871

Dear Sir

I have your letter ...

... held ... left ... to Ky = now is about ... vicinity ... the ... at Ala ... make visual ... in Mobile Alabama ... campaign ... for a tract of land.

He is a man ... allegince admirable in all ... a woman ...

[p. 13[1]]

... G. McWhorter of ... Elijah Clarke is collecting materials. Can ... his ancestor ... give you information of him. He ...

I think if you ...

[p. 13[2]]

Georgia you might learn much of their ... Col Williamson. Both Clarke & Williamson lived and died in that county.

The person most likely to know the people up by that country ... the revolution & Indian wars in that part of the country is Robert Coombs has merely a ... what noted ... in that country and has always lived there.

If you could get his ear, I do not doubt he could give you a great deal of local information. Wilson

[p. 13[3]]

Lumpkin, if living ... aged & excellent man & some twenty years ... told me he was collecting & recovering every ... the history of the State. The Early records of the Court and recording office are full of interest. The history of Georgia has never been written. The place was ... men ... the ... of its history ... full of interest.

Very Respectfully
J. A. Campbell

Lyman C. Draper Esq.
Madison Wisconsin

[p. 14]

169 St Paul Street
Balt. Octo 15 1872

My Dear Sir

I have recd your letters of the 1st Ult 7th Inst & your letter to Mrs Troutman, my cousin. My mother Mrs. Duncan G. Campbell was the youngest daughter and child of Col Micajah Williamson. She was born in Feb. 1793. Her father was then living & died while She was a child of two years old. He was buried on Little river about 8 miles fm Washington where he owned land & had mills. He was of Irish descent & settled near what is now Lynchburg Virginia then a wild country before the revolution. He married Salley Gilliam in Virginia & before the revolution settled in Wilkes County upon the site of the town of Washington.

[p. 14[1]]

His family was a large one. He reared five sons, Micajah, Charles Peter, William, Thomas. Six daughters Nancy — who married John Clarke Sally, who married John Griffin & afterwards Charles Tait — Susan who married Thompson Bird Patsey who married Thomas Fitch Betsey who married Peterson Thweatt & Mary (Polly) who married my father D. G. C.

Peter William Thomas & all the girls were born in Georgia.

My impression is that the family were all born in the state of Geo. Charles Williamson was the cotemporary of John Clarke & I think was the oldest son but of this I am not certain.

Micajah & he were the oldest boys & were old enough to be unfiet during the war

[p. 14²]

The county of Wilkes was at this time on the frontier. The Indian country, the Cherokees on the north & the Creeks on the South & South west approached very near to the border of the county. I am not sure that either Oglethorpe or any other of the boundary counties were laid out. Wilkes was a large & thinly settled district. The loyalists (tories) fled to the Indian nations and their half breeds that have become promanent in those tribes are generally refugees from the white settlements. A very curious fact came to my knowledge in respect to one of their c... — the younger brother of the Col Grierson who commanded in the British troops at Augusta during the war was trader near Augusta during the war. He absconded &

[p. 14³]

settled in the heart of the Indian nation (Creeks) near the Tallapoosa river in the Hillabees. He accumulated a great number of negroes & money there, & died about 1824, or 5.

He was the youngest of nine brothers all of whom died and the barony of Lagg descended to him shortly before his death. He left a daughter by an Indian woman about 18 years old. She married one of her own slaves & was removed across the Missi. r in 1836. Grierson was preparing to ... scattered when he died.

These tories were hostile and incited the Indians to hostilities. The war was ferocious and bloody. Nothing was spared either of life or of property.

[p. 14[4]]
2
the Georgia regiment in upper Georgia was commanded by Elijah Clarke. My grandfather (Micajah Williamson) was lieutenant Col.

Their office was to defend the settlements from these incursions.

The house of my grandfather was burnt. A price was offered for his head. His son Micajah was hung to extort from him information of his fathers place of concealment in presence of his mother.

He was cut down & left for dead but by his mothers care revived.

The family recollections were full of accounts of their abandonment of their home & their sufferings for want of food & fear of Indians. How that they lived on oats & berries &c &c.

The regiment went into South Carolina. I have no

[p. 14[5]]
means of reference, but I have an impression that they were at Musgrove's Mills, & some of them were at Kings Mountain.

The family tradition is that my grandfather lost a portion of his hand at the Cowpens — that the family consisting of the mother & children under the convoy of the sons, principally Charles reached the vicinity of the battle ground the day before, & that Charles went to the battle & that his father was made acquainted by seeing him fighting bravely of the proximity of his family.

Charles was described as a youth of 14.

This need not surprize you. In the late war

[p. 14[6]]
there were a number of instances of youths of that age who were attending their fathers & were active in fight & some cases where they ran away from home to have a share.

The size of Micajah Williamson was great. His sons were generally above six feet two inches, & William would probably reach to six feet four or five inches. He was industrious a good manager of property and left a large estate in lands and of slaves.

My mother was left 20,000 acres, not worth a great deal at that time.

His children spoke of him with great respect.

[p. 14[7]]
Peter Williamson his son, was a judge in Alabama & died about 1844, had a good recollection of him. He spoke of him as cool, methodical and undaunted. He spoke of Genl. Clarke as heroic, never going to a battle without receiving wounds & as an intense sufferer from physical pain. He spoke of them as a rare combination of men who aided one another so that each supplied what seemed to be necessary to efficient command so that together they were perfect.

I remember no personal anecdote except one

[p. 14[8]]
in reference to the Kettle creek battle.

He told me that the Tory commander Boyd was a man of ability. That the fight was unfavorable to the Whigs till Boyd fell. That three persons his father & two others whose names he mentioned were under him & without being aware of it were cut off from their lines & could not reach them. Discovering this they commencd to fire at Boyd who was at a distance.

All of them fired successively & the third shot was

his fathers & that Boyd fell & a panic ensued, and they escaped.

I do not remember if anything of this is in

[p. 14[9]]

any of the Georgia annals.

I suppose that Col Williamson was about fifty three or five years of age when he died. His widow died in 1814 at Washington Wilkes Co.

Gen E. Clarke lived about 12 miles & abov from Washington in Wilkes Co. & several of his children lived in that vicinity. My feeling is he was from North Carolina & that he settled in Georgia before the revolution. He had three sons of my acquaintance and a number of daughters. His wife died about 1825 in Wilkes a very old woman, but active and with her intellect in full vigor.

I have no doubt that Mrs. Campbells account of her fathers age is accurate.

[p. 14[10]]

He died at St. Andrews Bay in Florida in 1830, or 1831. I knew him well in 1828-9. He was then a vigorous man, engaged in making surveys of live oak in Florida under a commission from the U. S. My impression is that his obituary notice described him as aged 43, or 44. His wife my aunt died a few days after him.

Charles Williamson, my uncle, married Gen E. Clarkes daughter & died a few years after in Wilkes Co. He left a son, who was a Clergyman & died in Philadelphia a long time ago. The widow of Charles Willianson married Mr. Hobby who was editor of the Augusta Chronicle for many years & a man of culture and talent.

I do not know when Elijah Clarke died.

[p. 14[11]]
He is mentioned in a letter of McGilverey at p. 81, 2 that of Picketts history of Ala. In that or some other letter of McGilvery he speaks of Clark respectfully & with great contempt of every other Georgia officer.

In some of the American State papers, there are allusions to Gen Clarks erection of a separate state to the south of the Ogeechee & being in a sort of insurrection. I infer that he lived several years after the date of the letter of McGilvery.

This fact must be attainable in the Court of Ordinary of Wilkes Co. Mr. McWhorter could ...ain this.

I believe I have answered your inquiries.

Very Respectfully
J A Campbell

[p. 14[12]]

Addenda

These families were involved in the political & party strifes of Georgia until about the year 1830, when the politics of that State assumed the complexion ...ed from the National parties. After the war ended in 1783 the country remained disturbed for a number of years & the Indians were generally in a state of disturbance. When all this terminated there was a great immigration from Virginia. These immigrants brought wealth & more of education than the earlier settlers were able to procure. The local contests were betwen the Ante-revolutionary men & the New population.

Gen John Clarke formed a party. His brothers-in-law Griffin & Bird were men of ability

[p. 14[13]]
& at that time persons who were afterwards known to the

country. Forsyth, Walker Early && were his friends.

Wm. H. Crawford who was a Virginian was the leader of the other party & acquired ascendancy in the State as leader of the Jefferson party.

There was a duel between Gen Clarke & Crawford in which the latter was severely wounded. This personal bitterness continued till both parties died & gave a hue to the discussions. They were personal accrimonious & the statements of the one of the other are untrustworthy. They did not have power to make a fair judgement.

[p. 14[14]]
My father married in 1808, so that his connection with public affairs was long after the origin of these parties.

I knew Gen J Clarke in 1828-9. He had then removed to Florida. He was a man of great integrity. His word was truth. His intrepidity exceeded that of any person I ever saw. Prompt ready active, he seemed to have accomplished a result while other men only engaged in ascertaining what was to be done. He read the Bible, & hardly any other book. He read newspapers. He had but little cultivation.

Mrs. Campbell of Galvezton his daughter married my fathers brother. So our connexion is close by blood & affinity.

[p. 14[15]]
She was thoroughly educated & in the long struggles in the state the influence of her mother & herself, was very sensibly felt.

It is not often that women so commanding in stature, dignity, worth, & culture, were united with such winning manners overflowing courtesy & such gentleness and charity.

[p. 15]

723 St Paul street
Baltimore July 9, 1887

My Dear Sir,

I have your letter of the 24th Ult.

My impression is that General Elijah Clarke migrated to Georgia from Anson County North Caralina, before the revalutionary war commenced.

Their settlement in Wilkes County was on the south side of the Broad river.

When I first knew of them, several of the daughters of Gen Clark had married & residing there. Gen John Clark the son of Elijah was a resident in that county before the

[p. 15[1]]

beginning of this century.

Afterwards, he resided in Telfair county Baldwin Co & he died in Florida about 1833.

There is a portrait of Gen Elijah Clark in Mobile Alabama. He was taken with his uniform as a Genl. His countenance is that of a bold resolute determined man of a martial ease.

I can probably procure a photograph and the

[p. 15[2]]

facts that you ask for, with certanty.

I have read with great interest your history and will render such assistance as lies within my power. My address I have placed at the head of this letter.

Very Respectfully Yours
John A. Campbell

Lyman C. Draper Esq
Madison Wisconsin

[p. 16]
(illegible)

[p. 16[1]]
... The portrait

[p. 16[2]]
... made ... not till you have ... My noble & venerated grandfather, Genl E Clark will be fairly dealt with

[p. 16[3]]
... justice, will his last ...

[p. 17]

Mobile, March 26 1852

Mr. L. C. Draper
Sir

Your letter of the 13th Inst. has just been received and I regret that I cannot give you any information about my Grandfather and his family.

In my letter to Mr. McWhorter I told him everything I knew. He had very dark hair, almost black, his portrait has blue eyes and judging from it he was tall and fine looking. I do not know anything about the age of my Grandfather and Mother but suppose he was the oldest as I never heard it alluded to. The battles to which you refer I do not know anything about them. He had a

[p. 17[1]]
brother Lewis Clarke who moved to Natchez Mississippi soon after the State was settled and ... farming near that place ... where he ... only know that he was married in North Carolina and moved to Georgia. I do not know anything about the Ancestors except what you have heard

from Mr. McWhorter which I regret exceedingly. It would have afforded me great pleasure to have rendered you some assistance.

Very respectfully
E. M. Hobson

[p. 18]

Greensboro Oct 8th 1872

Mr. L. C. Draper
Dear Sir

Your letter of the 20th of Sep. has not been received on account of my being absent from Greensboro. Please accept many thanks for the book which you were so kind as to send me. I regret that, I did not receive it sooner, so that I could have acknowledged it before this. I am very much obliged, to you for it, and will read it at once.

I do not know, the age of my Grandfather or how old he was, when he died. I heard my Mother say, that I was about a year old, when he died.

[p. 18[1]]
I will be 73 in January. I do not know, where he was born but believe it was in North Carolina, from what I have heard my Mother say. My Grandfather & Grandmother were burried, in Lincoln Co Georgia, on their plantation. I never was at the grave yard and do not suppose, that there is a tombstone, over their graves as he died, before they were much used. Mr. McWhorter wrote me, that he intended to visit their graves, so as to ascertain their age, and the time of their death, if there were any gravestones.

I do not remember the year in which, my Uncle sen John Clarke died. He died at St Andrews Bay Florida.

[p. 18[2]]
Mrs. Ann W. Campbell his daughter, and Judge John A Campbell his Newphew, of New Orleans, can give you any information you wish to know about him, particularly in regard to his age and when he died. From them, I have no doubt, but what you can learn everything, in regard to his private life, as well as that of a soldier.

I never saw Micajah Williamson and do not recollect, ever to have heard the family speak of him. He was the Grandfather of Mrs. Campbell, being her Mother's Father. Also the Grandfather of Judge Campbell. Both of them, I presume know his history and would with pleasure, give you the desired

[p. 18[3]]
information.

Charles Williamson, I think was his son. I do not know when or where he died, but think that he was burried, at his home Wilkes or Lincoln Co. Georgia on his plantation. He was a year or two older, than I am which would make him, now about 74 or 75 years old.

There are only three of my Grandfathers, Grandchildren living. Mrs. Campbell, Denny Thompson and myself. Denny Thompson lives about twenty miles from Mobile. A letter directed to him, to the care of Judge Alexander McAinsley, Mobile I expect would reach him. Mr. Thompson has the portrait of my Grandfather, and the Photograph

[p. 18[4]]
which I will enclose to you was copied from an Ambrotype which was taken from the portrait. There was a letter of my Grandfathers, published in the Savannah paper, during the revolutionary war. I have tried to get it for you. I saw it in

the year, 1859 in New York. Mrs. Lee then had it. She is now dead. Her daughter Mrs. Roberts, had all of her papers and letters, and does not know, what became of it. I will write again and try to get it, if successful will either, send the letter to you or a copy of it.

My Fathers name was Edwin Mounger, and my Mothers

[p. 18[5]]

Fannie Clarke before her marriage. She was the sixth child.

I regret that I cannot give you more information, in regard to my Grandfather and his family. At any time if I can be of the, slightest service or render you any assistance, it will always afford me great pleasure. It gives me much pleasure, to recall the time when my Ancestors were living, so you need not fear, giving me the slightest trouble. I should be pleased to hear at your convenience, how you progress in your work, as I take a deep interest in it.

Very respectfully,
Your friend
E. M. Hobson

[p. 19]

Feb. ...
Houston Co Geo. ...

Mr. L. C. Draper
My dear Sir

... of you ... to ascertain facts ... the ... & do justice, to ...fer 50 ..., ... even early in ... my fathers manuscripts, in ... given you much valuable information respecting ...ard. I was 70 years old, ... think he only ... give you the desired information. I am sure that one of ... was younger than her husband ...

[p. 19[1]]
My father ...

My father died on the 12th & my Mother the 26th of ... 1832 and know that ...uments were applied for or received ... the benefit of the pensions act. You ... to ... that year. There is a no... directed to their ... which is answered ... of my fathers life. They died at their residence on St Andrews bay Jackson Co Florida a beautiful but secluded spot. I know of no town near there. The place was ...ion-ally sold & I have never

[p. 19[2]]
... able to recover it. My grandmother was 80 or perhaps older and died at her son in law's Mr. Josiah Grayson in ... Wilkes Co Geo. If ... all you ... nor do I know anything as to the age of Micajah Williamson or when he died. My cousin Mrs. Baber, like myself has heard the ... our grand-mother's brother Gov Clark ... to ... yours ... of his sons ... It ... I wrote regarding Col. Edward Clark ... is to ... & all in this to be. his Mother is 85 and with her visit he ... her memory is not reliabel her statements being too discon-nected to be of any service. My grandfather died before my birth but I remember hearing some woman Say my

[p. 19[3]]
... engage... British ... her ... my daughter that ... me that ... and that since all ... was in ... of the Tories & her ... of their old ... how savage ... I would have ... I later heard ... the ... But regrets are vain & ... other ... duties are demanded it ... & are ... for the task.

Your earnest wishes ... the ... will ... With high Esteem ... see his ... Mrs. ...

I enclose ... of the firm Parker & ... Galveston ... will forward with a photograph likeness of my grandmother

& father.

[p. 19[4]]
"Cor...ion conec... ...pedia ..."

"Clark E... an American General born in ... Casab... died near the ...ent Ge... He removed to Georgia in 1770 became a captain in 1771 distinguished ... in ... frontiers, ... a colonel ...

he defeated the ... musgroves ... & ... & ... to the ... in 1780. He ... many ... several treaties with the Creek Indians.

The above ...

[p. 19[5]]
... be a ...

John Clark son of Elijah Clark & Hannah his wife born Feb 28th 1766 Died Oct. 12th 1832. This is taken ... the family record.

[p. 20]

Greensboro Oct 23rd.

Mr. L. C. Draper
Dear Sir

Your letter of the 13th Inst has been received, and regret that I know so little about my family. I was so young I presume, I have heard a great many things about them, which made no impression on me. I hope that you can get some information from Mr. Thompson, but am afraid he will know very little. The Photograph which I sent you, of my Grandfather is a good one, it is very much like the portrait, which was said to be a fine likeness. He had deep blue eyes and dark chestnut colored hair. I have not heard

[p. 20[1]]
from Col. Edward Clarke in several years, he was then living in Austin Texas. If he has moved from there, perhaps the Post-Master can give you his address. I wrote by todays mail, to Mr. Abner P. Blocker of Austin, to know if he was still living there if so will write, to you as soon as I hear from him. Col Edward Clarke's Father moved to New Orleans, Lousiana when Edward was a small boy and he never lived, near his relations. His Father died when he was a child. Mrs. Edward Thomas of Augusta Georgia is a Granddaughter, of Lewis Clarke, perhaps she can tell you something about him. I heard she had a son named after her Grandfather. He had a Grandson who lived in this place. Mr.

[p. 20[2]]
Hutchinson, a Methodist minister. He died several years ago, leaving a Widow and several children but they do not know, anything about the family. Charles Clarke I expect was his son. I do not know how many children he had. I knew two of his daughters; they are now dead. I do not know where his descendants are living.

My Cousin, Charles Williamson moved to Philadelphia, when he was a young man. He was a Presbyterian Minister, and married but I do not know whether he had any children or not. I heard several years ago, that he was dead. I believe I wrote to you that Mrs. Ann W. Campbell's Mother was a daughter of Micajah Williamson, she may know something about Charles Williamson.

[p. 20[3]]
Micajah Williamson had a son of the same name. Mrs. Campbell was a daughter, of Gen John Clarke and she can give you some information. My Grandfather must have been, more than 26 years old when the Revolution com-

menced, as my Mother was the sixth child and she was born during the war. My Grandfather I expect was of course older than my Grandmother. My Uncle John Clarke, I expect was very young at the commencement of the war. There was a creek either in Lincoln or Wilkes Co, named Jack Creek after him. There was a place called Clarks Station, where my Grandfather and his men were stationed. I heard my Mother say that my Uncle John Clarke, was crossing a creek with his

[p. 20[4]]

5

men, the Indians fired on them from the woods, where they were concealed. One man was mortally wounded and fell from his horse. He beged for water, while he dying. My Uncle ran to the creek and got some water, in his hat and gave it to him.

I regret that I cannot answer all of your questions, but hope that you can get the desired information from others. It would afford me great pleasure, to assist you and am sorry that I am not better posted, in regard to my ancestors. I wish you great success and hope that you will ascertain, everything necessary to complete your book, without much trouble.

Very respectfully your friend
E. M. Hobson.

[p. 21]

Philadelphia ...

Mr. Lyman C. Draper
Dear ...

... returned ... Campbell a pleasant ... enclosed to my cousin ... that his Mother may ... respecting the ... <u>which I ...</u>

I am under the impression that ... whom I perfectly remember when My Grandfather had two Children

[p. 21[1]]
... their sons ... the 20 years ... sister ... George Few ... for him ... the husband ... mother. My Mothers ... place in ... He ... His obituary was ... you, substantially gave opinion ... when made a Capt.

Please return ... me ... you my Fathers photography. We all regret that the ... being a little ... & ... both photographs were ... but we did our best. ... tell me he has the

[p. 21[2]]
history you so kindly sent me in good keeping; ... have it in a few days, and provide myself much pleasure in its perusal, having been more than interested in the former volume, for all of which I beg you will accept my most grateful thanks.

Most respectfully
Your obliged friend
Mrs. Ann W Campbell

Direct to Galveston
Ca...

... was ... paper ...ville Georgia

[p. 22]
Gen. John Clark, of Georgia, died on 12th Oct. 1832, at his residence on St. Andrew's Bay, West Florida, formerly of Georgia, in the 67th year of his age. On the 30th Septr., while engaged in the duties of the live-oak agency, he was attacked with bilious fever on St.Vincent Island, & was carried thence in a small Sloop to his residence on St Andrew's Bay, where he lingered a few days.

During the Struggle of the Revolution, he usually

attended his father, the gallant Col. Elijah Clarke, and participated in the many skirmishes and battles in which that active partisan was engaged. At the age of fourteen, the subject of this notice was sent to school in Wake County, North Carolina, where he did not long remain, before a scouting party being raised to go against the Tories and British, he joined them; and after his return from the Expedition, finding an opportunity of company to the place where he left his father, he abandoned his school. He again joined his father in the ranks of his countrymen, and fought under him at the last siege of Augusta. At the age of sixteen he was appointed Lieutenant, and then Captain of Militia. In 1786 he was elected Major, and in that capacity he commanded, in 1787, under his father in the battle fought at

[p. 22[1]]

Jacks Creek with the Indians. He rose in rapid succession, through different grades, until he was chosen Brigadier General, and then Major General by the Legislature. He was Sheriff, & then representative, & then Senator in the State Legislature, from Wilkes County. Near the close of the war of 1812-'15 at a most critical period, the command of all the forces destined for the protection & defence of the Sea-coast and southern boundary of Georgia was given him by Gov. Early. In 1816, he was elected to the Legislature, Presidential Elector, and afterwards twice honored with the office of Governor of the State. He filled also several other commissions and appointments from the Legislature & Governor of the State.

In 1827 he removed to West Florida, and sought a retreat from the cares and turmoils of busy life, on the secluded borders of St. Andrew's Bay, where he had hoped to spend the evening of his life in the enjoyment of domestic quiet and repose. The Expenses incident to the settlement of a new country, soon rendered it necessary for him again to embark in active business, & he accepted the appointment of agent for the protection of live oak. His wife Ann Clark died of bilious cholic, on 26th Oct. 1832, in the fifty (?) ninth year of her age.

Somewhat abbreviated from the "Floridian", 30th Oct. 32.

[p. 23]

Greensboro Dec 9th/72

Mr.Draper
Dear Sir

Soon after the reception of your last letter, I wrote to Austin Texas, to try and learn something about Col Ed Clarke, and have just received an answer to my letter. He has left Austin and g... in the fall, in the Eastern part of Texas. He was Lt Governor of Texas in 1861, when Gen. Sam. Houston was Govenor, and when Houston was removed, he was elected or appointed in his place. He served, until his term expired and then joined the Southern Army as Lt. Col, in Col

[p. 23[1]]

George Flouronys regiment.

He married a Miss Evans and his family, lived in ... during the war and after the ..., he moved with them to Marshall. I regret that I Could not learn more about him. Perhaps he is still, living there and you can ascertain, from him or his family, all you wish to learn.

Very respectfully
Your friend
E. M. Hobson

[p. 24]

Edward Clark. Gen. Elijah Clark's death & age

Marshall Texas,
Nov 6th 1872.

Lyman C. Draper,
Madison Wisc

My Dear Sir. Your letter of the 27th ult was recieved the latter part of last week. The book & pamphlets a mail or two after. I am greatly obliged to you for them. I shall find much pleasure in perusing them I am sure, as I see they contain much of such litrature as I am fond of reading.

Your former communications were not received, & it is only through Mrs Campbell that I had before heard of your proposed life of Genl. Sumter, & your desire for information touching the history of my Grdfather Genl Elijah Clark. In answer to her, I sent such data as I could furnish, &, until your letter came, I had supposed my answer had gone safely to her.

In answer to your inquiries I state: My mother does not know the birth place of Genl E Clark, or the date of his birth. She neither recollects the date of his death. On the inside of a large gold ring which was my father's there is this inscription, "Dec'd

[p. 24[1]]

Decr. 1799, aged 57." & this, my mother tells me refers to the death & age of Grd Father. This, I presume, is correct.

My mother cannot give the age of my Grd mother, when she died.

She does not know the age of Gov. John Clark when he died. She thinks he reached about the age of his father, but this I think is mere conjecture. From circumstances in my own recollection, I think he died in, or about the summer of 1831. From family tradition I know that he was very early in life in active military service. I have often heard of some Creek in Georgia taking the name, "Jacks Creek," from his having fought & won a battle upon it, & this may be the battle to which you allude as, "Musgroves Mills."

My mother mentions two brothers of Genl E. Clark. One named Lewis, older than the Genl, the other Gipson & younger. They resided somewhere about Port Gibson Miss. She knows nothing now of any of their descendants. Gov. Clark, Gov. of Miss. before the recent war, & a Genl. in said war, is very likely, I think, a descendant of one of these brothers. I do not know his address.

My mother knows nothing of Genl Clark's parents, & if he had sisters she does not know it.

[p. 24[2]]
She knew a Col Micajah Williamson in Ga. but does not know when he died or his age. She has a very imperfect recollection of hearing of some woman giving my Grd father notice of the approach of the British before some battle in which he was engaged, but her memory is so indistinct that she can state nothing about it.

The first book in which I ever saw mention of my Grd father in connection the Revl. war, was a novel, entitled, "Horse-Shoe Robinson, & there, in the battle of "Kings Mountain". In White's notes I have seen a more extended account of his services, & in Lippincotts history of Ga. shool perces, you will find a more complete history of him, than any source I have any knowledge of. It is more than probable, however, that you are familiar with these books.

I think it very likely you may obtain information

which will be of some service, from Hon John H Campbell, formerly Asst Just Sup Court U. S. He now resides in the City of Baltimore I believe, & has also, I think, a law office in the City of New Orleans. I feel assured that he can afford you some assistance in your inquiries.

I regret that I cannot better aid you in the work in which you are engaged. In the

[p. 24[3]]
very scanty information I send, I trust however, there may be found a clue which will lead you to something valuable.

If I can further serve you in any way, I shall be pleased to do so.

Very respectfully & truly yours
Edward Clark

[p. 25]

Augusta Ga May 5th/74

Sir

By request of My Mother in Law Mrs Edw Thomas I have you enclosed a Memorandum Made by Mrs E in her own hand writing in accordance with the request contained in Your Communication at the 28th Oct.

Mrs T requests me also acknowledge Receipt of a copy of History of Wisconsin.

It is very probably that you may get some information in addition to that given by Mrs T. by corresponding with Geo G McWhorter Esq. of this

[p. 25[1]]
City.

Very Resp. Yours
B. F. Hall

P. S. It will afford me much pleasure to assist you in amy

Way in my power in your undertaking and should be pleased to hear from you at any time on the subject.

B. F. H.

[p. 26]

M... Edward Thomas
Augusta Geo
Oct 5, 1872

General Elijah Clarke ... my grandfather Louis Clark ... Genl Elijah Clarke died in 1799 in Wilkes County. Pr... my grandfather ... Mississippi ... 50 ... in 1820. Louis Clark never had ... he died quite young he was marr... but his family are all dead. Genl Elijah Clark's farm ... was 15 miles ... George G. McWhorter

[p. 26[1]]
profession a lawyer.

I have two sisters both living in Alabama. One of them had ... My grandmothers family left Georgia but unfortunately about four years ago ... was burned and everything lost. Genl Elijah Clarke was older than my grandfather

[p. 27]

Macon March 11th 1873

...

[p. 27[1]]
an old family ... family. The family record of ... an exact copy of it. It is perfectly reliable & ... the fear of ... the fear of his removal to ... State, nor of his place of ... accept the Volume which accompanies this letter to them ... of the City ... native Georgian, who though advanced in age, still possesses much of the sprightliness of ... years Judge L. Q.

C. Lamar, mentioned in the work, was my first husband. Our son, (his Father namesake) is also mentioned. He though quite young, was a member of

[p. 27[2]]
... daughter such for ... am possibly ... of Judge Campbell ... ... information which ... the act of ... valuable State History of ... G. Hutman ... can obtain ... of ...

[p. 27[3]]
of ... from my Son M. L. Lamar of, Oxford, Mississippi.

[p. 28]
120
... on the ... both ... March 1751 ... 1765.

	1766
	March 23, 1768
	Feb. 17, 1770
Peter	Feb. 25, 1772
...	Jan. 6th 1774
...	... 30, 1776
	... 1779
	Nov. 14, 1781
...	Dec 14, 1783
	Feb. 23, 1786
John William	April 14, 1790
...	May 17, 1793
...	
...	... 1800.
...	... 1804.
...	

The above ...

[p. 29]
Ex Gov Clark of Miss.

Natchez Miss. May 20, '72

Mr. Lyman Draper
Madison Wisconsin

Dear Sir,

I had the honor to receive your letter of 4th inst. Since its recpt I have made inquiry of some of our oldest citizens. No one has any picture or recollection of Col. John Winn. I know one of his grand sons, now died, also a widow of one of his sons, who was related to the Wests & Greens, & also knew Col. Cowley Mead & Gen Hinds but only as a boy knows old men. None of these old families are living but in the third & fourth generation of the associates of Col. Winn.

I today enclose your letter to Col. James S. Johnson, of Church Hill, Jefferson Co, Miss, who has resided in that Co for some forty years. He is a gentleman of intelligence Connected by Marriage with the oldest families there, & I think has preserved some memorials of the old Spanish times.

[p. 29[1]]

I will ask him to correspond with you. I lost during the late war a copy of a gossiping old book written by Ellicott, the U. S. Commissioner appointed after the Spanish treaty of ... of Oct 1795 to take possession of the ceded territory. He was much annoyed by the a... of Spain here, but the Green, ... the old families of Jefferson were with him & he gives the history of many of these old settlers. I think it refers to Col Winn. I recollect that he refers often to the Greens & Woods &c. I think it was of him some one gave the "sentiments" at a dinner table "He has hunted our Hinds, haunted our Woods & fed upon our

Meads & Greens". But it has been many years since I looked into the book & nothing of value remains in my memory. I think there is a copy ("Ellicotts Journal") at Jackson Miss, if so Judge W. L. Sharkey (late provisional Gov. of Miss) can find it. Gov. Sharkey indeed is the only

[p. 29[2]]

man living that I can now think of who would probably have any memory of Col. Winn, & he would write you. His address is Jackson, Miss.

Very respectfully &c
Chas Clark

[p. 30]

Natchez Miss. Feby 12, 1873

Lyman C Draper Esq Madison Wisconsin

Dear Sir,

On my return home last week I found your letter of 13th ult.

I regret that I can give you no information in regard to Gen. Elijah Clark. I was not of his family or descendts. My ancestors were of Maryland. My father father was a soldier in the Revolution & several times wounded but never rose beyond the rank of sergeant.

I knew Elija L Clark of Claiborn Co. near Port Gibson Miss. & think I have seen Gibson Clark. I send your letter to Col. Jno H. Coleman of Port Gibson with request to make inquiry & answer it.

I am very respectfully
Your obdt Ret &c
Chas Clark

[p. 31]

Port Gibson Miss. May 31, 1873.

Lyman C. Draper Esq. }
Madison, Wisconsin } Dear Sir:

Your Favor of 24th Inst. was received on Saturday night last, as was also the volume on the history of Wisconsin, for which please accept my acknowledgment.

Some ten days ago I recd. a letter from Gov. Charles Clark, enclosing yours to him of Jany. 13, and requesting me to endeavor to obtain and forward to you any information I could get upon this subject. Elijah L Clarke died in this county many years ago, and my impression is that all his family have removed to other states, mostly, I think, to Texas. His younger brother Charles B. Clarke still resides in this county about 22 Miles from Town, and is in the habit of occasionally visiting Port Gibson.

As soon as I received Gov. Clark's letter, I wrote a few lines to Charles B. stating that I wanted to see him the next time he came here, and requesting him to call at my office, and left my letter with his merchant here to be sent out to him by the first opportunity, and I learn this morning that it was sent by one of his neighbors, the week before last. He has not been in town since, but I am satisfied he will call on me the first time he comes to town. As soon as I see him, I will communicate to you all the information he can give me. if he has none himself, he may possibly be able to put us on the track of getting it elsewhere.

At all events, you shall hear from me as soon as I shall have seen him.

Yours Very Respy. &c.
Jno. R. Coleman

[p. 32]

Milledgeville Geo 14 Jany 1872

My Dear Sir

Col Wm. Candler Moved from The Neighbourhood many years ago and settled near Natches on the Mississipie and died thare. I know him well. our County records was burnt here many years ago.

Henry and Richard Hampton, are both dead. Their Brother Genl Wade Hampton at ... South Carolina can tell uall about them.

Col McGraff went to Mississ... with Candler and died thare. Col Williamson died many years ago, and I think ... a Son ... in Milledgeville Ga.

Very many thanks My Dear Sir for the Phamphlets.

It will give me pleasure to serve you in any way in my power. please command my services.

Most Respectfully
Yr. Obt Sevt
John S. Thomas

I think I ... a small Book written by Genl Frank Marion of South Carolina on the Revolutionary War. If I can find it, I will send it to you.

[p. 33]

ORDINARY'S OFFICE
OF
Baldwin County, Ga.,

Milledgeville, Feb. 17, 1872.

Captain Micajah Williamson was one of the first settlers in Wilkes County, and died there; he commanded a company in the Revolutionary War, and lost a finger at the battle of Kettle Creek, he served through the war.

... can ... McGriff sister in ... & Spain. ...

[p. 34]

Col. Micajah Williamson.

Milledgeville Ga Feb 26th 1872

Col Thomas

At your request I give you all the information about my grandfathers (Col. Micajah Williamson) revolutionary services that I am in possession of. His biography is that he first served as a Captain the Brigade he was in was commanded by Elijah Clark afterwards Major Gen E. Clark at the siege of Augusta or at the battle of Guilford he was raised to Lieutenant Col: he was afterwards wounded loosing his little finger at the battle of Kettle Creek, Wilkes County, Ga.; he was afterwards in many battles with the tories and Indians until his eldest son, who married the daughter of Gen E. Clark, took his place in command of the Georgians. Col Charles Williamson. I am sorry that I am not able to give you at this time a fuller detail of his services, and the many hardships endured by him and his followers. Respectfully

W. T. Williamson

[p. 35]

ORDINARY'S OFFICE

OF

Baldwin County, Ga.,

Milledgeville, Feb. 26th 1872

Col J S Thomas

Dr Sir

In answer to your requests relative to Col Richard McGriff I know little about his services as a revolutionary patriot but have often heard my father speak of him in the very highest terms as one of that band who served with my granfather Micajah Williamson during the war he lived to be an old man but where he died I am not certain. But I think he died in Pulaski County Georgia. This Band of revolutionary heroes were the men that caused Wilkes County Georgia to be called during the War and up to this day the Hornets nest. I cannot state for a certainty what grade he ranked in as an Officer whether Lieutenant Captain or Major though he was always stiled Majr McGriff while living. Yours Respectfully

W. T. Williamson

Col John S Thomas
Milledgeville Ga

[p. 35[1]]

2/ 1152
| 576
72
4
288
2
576

[p. 36]

Near Milledgeville Sept. 14th 1872

Dear Sir,

I received your letter making some enquiries relative to Col McGriff and my grandfather Micajah Williamson. I have endeavoured to ascertain for your benefit all about Col. McGriff. I knew the old man but cannot find out where he died, as he left this place, and as well as I now remember, moved to Hawkinsville, Pulaski County Ga.; and went from there west and died. I know of but one man that can rightfully tell or give you correctly the desired information; and I have not been able to see him since I received your letter, but when I see him I will get what information he is in possession of, and send it to you forthwith. My grandfather died before I was born consequently all the information I give you is traditional my father was one of the first graduates of Franklin College Athens Ga he lived to the extreme age of 83 years and retained his memory to the last from him I learned the most I shall be able to write you about his father. my father died July 1864. Micajah Williamson was a Virginian, But was one of the earliest settlers of Georgia; he settled in Wilkes

[p. 36[1]]

County and was the first squatter where Washington a beautiful village and and county capitol now stands it was, that is the County of Wilkes against the British indians and tories so hot a hole that it received the name of hornets nest my grandfather uncle Charles Williamson or John Clark in command of the Americans in all these skirmishes he, my g. father, was born in the same County that Thos Jefferson was he had 12 children. John Clark, who was a son of Genl Elijah Clark, Married my aunt Ann, the eldest daughter, and Capt Charles Williamson married the elder daughter of Elijah Clark. John Clark was Governor of this State several times; his eldest daughter married J. W. Campbell, and is now living, a widow, in Galveston, Texas; she was said to be one amongst the most intellectual women in the State. She possibly can and no doubt will, with much pleasure, give you all the aid she can, in your laudable enterprize. She is my senior by ten years. I have another cousin living in Macon Ga. her name is Mrs Sarah Troutman; she is very intelligent and probably can give you some valuable information relative to our grandfather; her address Mrs Sarah Troutman, Macon, Ga, care of Hiram Troutman Esqr. Col Peterson Thweatt, Atlanta Ga is another Cousin. Judge John A. Campbell now of N. Orleans, who was one of the Justices of the

[p. 36[2]]
U. S. Supreme Court But at the commencement of the war resigned is another Cousin. his mother was the youngest child of my grandfather; his father, Duncan G Campbell, was one of the first men in Ga in point of talent, and at the time of his death was the most prominent candidate for Governor of this State. My Gd. father entered the revolutionary army a Capt from Ga. and rose or was promoted to Col. At the siege of Augusta Ga., he commanded the American forces, Genl. Clark being sick, he was wounded at the battle of Guilford and afterwards lost a little finger at the battle of Kettle Creek, Wilkes County, Ga. My six aunts were all very tall majestic looking women 3 brunettes and 3 fair. they all married men of eminent abilities in their professions. My grandfather was about six feet one inch in height dark skin with large black eyes hair very black remarkably strait. You will find a description which is very complimentary to the Williamson family in Sparks history 50 Years in Middle Ga is the title. Capt Charles Williamson, the eldest son of my G father, died soon after peace was made he left but one child he was a son and named for his father, Charles: my last accounts of him he was preaching in Philadelphia a Presbyterian Minister: Uncle Charles commanded at the battle of Jacks Creek a company of cavalry he was with Col Dooly.

[p. 36[3]]
Thinking you might like to have the names of the children of Micajah Williamson I will give them to you in rotation and who they married.

Charles	married Miss Clark	
Ann	"	Gen John Clark
Sarah		Judge John Griffin
		2nd husband Judge Tait

Peter	married 5 times was a lawyer and preacher of the Methodist persuasion	
Micajah		Miss Early
Jefferson	died young	
Martha		Mr Fitch consul to the Floridas when he died at St Augustine
Susan		Dr T. Byrd
William W.		Miss Terrell
Elizabeth		P Thweatt Esqr
Mary		D G Campbell Esqr

one not named before it died

The males of this family were none of them under six feet 3 or four inches and one reached six feet six inches. The females were all tall remarkable for beauty and expressive faces. Theire form symmetry itself I must close this lest you consider me egotistical.

Respectfully yours W. T. Williamson

NB You shall hear from me If I can gather anything worth reporting about Col McGriff. I dont believe I told you in this that my grandfather died at his mill-place, Little river, Wilkes County Ga. 10 mls from Washington.

WTW

[p. 37]

Near Milledgeville Sept 30th 1872

Dear Sir

Yours came safe to hand and in compliance with your request hasten to give you such other information as I have been able to gather since I wrote last my Grandfather, Micajah Williamson died some time in 1789. Micajah Jr never had any issue; left no child; his wife was an Early, a family of much distinction in Ga. It has been many years since I heard from Charles W., the preacher; his mother, after the death of my uncle, married Mr Hobby, the former editor of the Augusta Chronicle and Sentinel, by whom she had several children; they are scattered and dead. There was one of them a Clerk to some Office in Washington City when last heard from by me. My uncle John Griffin left no child; his widow married Judge Tait, Griffins competitor in life, and successor as Judge of the Northern district of Ga; they left no child. Thos. Fitch that married my aunt Martha and was sent Consul to the Floridas by Mr. Monroe, carried his Nephew by marriage, John Bird, as his Secretary; they were located at St Augustine, where all died in one week's time with yellow fever. John Bird was then the only living son of Dr Thompson Bird and aunt Susan Williamson.

[p. 37[1]]
Mrs Troutman, of Macon, Ga., is the only one living of that branch of the family; she, I think, is some seventy years old. I am the son of W. W. Williamson; I have several half brothers and one own and one half sister living; my father died on the 8th day of July, 1864, at the advanced age of 83; his children are with me that youngest Just 15 years old. Uncle Peter Williamsons children, I think, are nearly all dead or moved west, I cannot tell where. I have not said where my Grandfather died at. He died in Wilkes County, Ga, ten miles from Washington, the County site, at his mill place in little River, the place is known by the old maps of Ga as Williamson's Mills. I will try and get you a volume of Sparks' fifty years in Middle Ga. Col Sparks lives in Louisiana, but has a brother G. O Sparks, and a Nephew who is an able man by the name of Hardeman; either of them can give you the P. O. of Col.Sparks, the author; they live in Macon Ga. I do not know his address. You may want my age. I was born on Kettle Creek, Wilkes County,

Ga, on the 8th day of December 1810. Albemarle is the county where my grandfather lived before coming to Ga I have often heard my father speak of Charlotte the town in Albemarle they used to abbreviate the name by leaving of the ville in speaking of the town I have learned

[p. 37[2]]
from good authority that Col. McGriff died in Macon Ga come time about the year 'forty; he became in his later days very intemperate and died in one of those Bacchanalian frolics somewhere near the time I give you. This I learned from a door neighbor of his. I hope you will excuse these unconnected sentences, for I am little accustomed to writing letters or anything else. I am an humble farmer that mixes but little with the world since the war. I will simply add that Griffin and Fitch that married two of my aunts were both Northern men. I shall be more than thankful for the volume of your work in the meantime additional items I may be able to glean I will with pleasure send them to you. I trust you may receive a letter from Mrs Ann Campbell, of Galveston Texas; she is more than 10 years my Sr, and as her father, Genl. John Clark was in most of the battles and skirmishes during the conclusion of the Revolution she can no doubt give you an interesting biography of all those that figured in those contests.

Yours truly,

W. T. Williamson

L. C. Draper Esqr.
Madison Wis

[p. 37[3]]
I think I stated my grandfather died in 98 if so it was wrong he died in 1789 W T W

[p. 38]

... Ga. Sept 30th 1872

... C. Draper

Dear Sir

I have received your communication ... my Grandfather, Col Williamsons ... of a ... of ... my Grandfather settled at ... Wilkes Co. Geo., Nov 5, 1719, for ... that ... my Mother was born in Wilkes Co, as registered in my fathers family Bible. The Time of his death must have been between the years 1792 & 93. ... child was born in 92 and his father died while she was still an infant.

[p. 38[1]]

... from her. Then, from ... of our family ... something of him ... as he was one of the judges of the Supreme Court of the U States previous to the late war.

... at present ... He practiced Law both ... & ...

Should I ascertain any facts in connection with my Grandfather which may be at all useful to you I will transmit them with pleasure to you. He left a large family, five sons and six daughters but

[p. 38[2]]

... G. Campbell ... gratification that ... Grandfather's ... so much ... oblig... his services in behalf of his country appreciated. Accept my thanks for your efforts ... thro' me, those of all his descendants. My Cousin Mrs John W. Campbell, can give you all necessary information concerning her Father, Gen John Clark, & her Grandfather Colo. Elijah Clark. Wishing for the most satisfactory success in your valuable undertaking, and earnestly requesting to be a subscriber to your History

Believe me to be

Respectfully ...
Fr. Troutman

[p. 39]

Near Milledgeville Nov 16th 1872

Dear Sir

Your letter was received in due course of mail and should have been replied to right away But that I was taken down with a severe spell of fever which came near killing me I am yet weak and feeble from its effects. My Cousin Mrs Troutman is some ten years my senior and I suppose her reccollection about the age of our forfathers are more reliable than mine And I am of the opinion that my Aunt Mrs Campbell carried with her the old family Bible she being the youngest child of my Grandfather. There is no tombstone that marks the grave. My grand mother was Sarah Gillum; they were married in Virginia, and moved from thence to Wilkes Co. Ga.; and both died in that County. I can recollect my grandmother well; she was very tall. I think it possible that you may get some valuable information from Mrs Sarah Chandler of Mobile: she is the sister of Judge Campbell and his sr by some years she is several years my Sr I am 62 the 8th day of Dec next.

[p. 39[1]]

We carried Georgia for Mr Greeley but all to no purpose we cannot overcome the monied aristocracy the united opposition of Banks Rail roads and other combinations and monopolies we will henceforth stand aloof and let the radicals have it their own way we can and will hold the balance of power once they begin to split up Yours truly

W. T. Williamson

Lyman C Draper
Madison Wis

[p. 39[2]]

Near Milledgeville March 5th 1873.

Dear Sir

Your kind favor has been recived with many thanks I will state to you that no one hear knows anything of Patrick McGriff I am Certain the one I know was familiarly known and called Dick The Dunlaps are our relatives by my Grand Mothers side Richard Dunlap of Tennessee was a man of some considerable eminence his residence or Post Office I am not able to give you as it has been some considerable time since I heard of him My Grand Mother was a Gillum Sarah Gillum was her maiden name She was very tall blue eyes was I suppose 60 or 65 when she died She died in 1813 in Wilkes County Ga I believe now I have answred to the best of my reccollection the last questions in your request. Yours truly

W T Williamson

L. C. Draper Esqr

[p. 40]

Milledgeville Geo.
Sept ...

My ... Sir,

... Col John Clarke ... Elijah Clarke & Colo John Clark ... long since ... Clark, ...ther Mrs John W Campbell & ... Campbell who m... [mistaken sir]

...

[p. 40[1]]

...

... New Orleans his ... office ... John W Campbell decd. ... to Mrs. ...nay Campbell who was the ...

... their f... cl... my ... that ...

[p. 40[2]]
... ...ans & Tories to ... energy and intrepidity, when ... s...ted ...ed for ... has ... their terms ...

[p. 40[3]]
plunder ...

... was taken ... Genl Smiths policy to ...

[p. 41]

Atlanta Geo Oct 23 1872

Lyman C. Draper

Madison Wis.

My dear Sir

While absent for d... yours of the 20th ult came here, and I intended replying sooner, but other pressing matters have caused me to neglect it.

I regret very much that I cannot give you much information relative to my Grand Father Col. Micajah Williamson. All of his children are dead, and I know of none of his grand Children that would likely know anything of his military & other History, unless it be the Hon John H Campbell (former Judge of the Supreme Court U. S.) now residing in New Orleans & practicing law.

... since I was 12 years of age & was trown upon my own resources for support, became a Printer then Editor, & was elected Comptroller ... 1855 & national in 1865. Having been engaged in

[p. 41[1]]
the Editorial, and other political life, and not having been fortunate enugh to make more than a comfortable support, which required all my time, I have never had the ... I had the taste, to hunt up or treasure up the deeds of my Ancestry.

As to Gov. Clark he had when he was a boy, and as my Father through a brother-in-law, was a Troup man vs Clarke, I never felt enough interest in him to learn much his history.

Mr Dunlap, former Comptroller General of Tennessee, is a descendant of the Williamson family, and I learned from my sister, (Mrs ... Bills, Montgomery, Alabama) not long since, that he had been gathering up "things of the past" about them but my dear sir, for causes above first stated, have taken no interest in such things & I am therefore truly sorry, I cannot gratify you with something worth putting in your Book.

Very truly yours
P Thweatt

No fronte

[p. 42]

Col. Wm. Candler, of Georgia.

Senate Chamber U. S.
March 31, 1871

Lyman C. Draper Esq
Dear Sir

I enclose you a letter from Mr. Candler ... Georgia in regard to ... grand-father in reply to your letter to me. Hoping it will be of some value to you, I am very respectfully

Your obt. Servant
Joshua Hill

[p. 43]

Gainesville Ga Mar 18th 1871

Hon Joshua Hill
Dear Sir

Yours of the first of January addressed to Hon

Milton A. Candler and referred by him to me for answer making inquiry concerning Col Candler of the revolution of 1776 has been received and would have been answered earlier but for my continued absence from home. I regret that my information concerning the revolutionary history of Col Wm Candler is quite meager. He was however my paternal grandfather but died when I was quite an infant as did my father also. All the information I have of him is derived from his son and my uncle Henry Candler who entered the service in his fathers Regiment early in the war and who was promoted in the same regiment successively to the positions of Lieutenant Captain and Major. He lived to a ripe old age and

[p. 43[1]]

died in what is now Bibb county. I was a man when he died and was on terms of intimacy with him. From him I have learned that my Grandfather William Candler of whom you enquire was the son of an English Merchant whose mame was also William Candler and who resided in Belfast Ireland. On the death of the father in Belfast my William Candler and his brother Zachariah fell heir to a small estate and with it emigrated to Virginia and settled in that colony when William was married to Elizabeth Anthony. After residing in Virginia a short time the two brothers becoming dissatisfied with their location Zachariah removed to North Carolina and William to Georgia and settled near Savannah, (Oct. 7, 1771, Wm. Candler, as D. S. [Dep. Surveyor) signed the oath of Allegiance. — White's Histl. Colln. of Georgia, p. 40) where he resided at the commencement of the revolutionary war. When hostilities began, having been from the beginning of the troubles an ardent supporter of the rights of the colonies, he raised and equipped principally at his own expense a regiment of mounted men known as Candlers minute men. Their field of operation was mainly Georgia and South Carolina. When campaigning they were under the command of Genl Sumter but much of the time they acted independently.

[p. 43[2]]

When no imminent danger threatened the most of the regiment was suffered to go to their homes to cultivate their farms only a few men being left at suitable points up and down the Savannah river to observe the approach of the enemy and to attend to their signal lights on the approach of danger. By means of these lights they were warned of danger and repaired as quickly as possible to their rendez-vous. They were thus enabled to render ... valuable service to the country and at the same time support their families. So obnoxious did Col. Wm. Candler ... the British ... that his mame was inserted in ... against ... out of the British parliament ... was leveled. He refusing to ... by that all his property which was considerable was seized and ... reduced to ashes by the British in the ... was designated as a ...") ...ficient in strategy ... but if forced to retreat had ... was said to maintain

[p. 43[3]]

his ground with the utmost tenacity. An anecdote is related of him that at one time when pursuing a party of tories he was drawn into an ambuscade and found himself confront-ing a large body of British troops. After an obstinate resistance finding himself completely overpowered instead of relieving himself by a movement to the rear he concen-trated his troops and made a sudden charge on the ... flank routing ..., and thus ... conditions made his escape and always ...uition he ... to the day of his death. He was ... did during the war and on ... was left on it ... as dead but was never captured.

After the termination of the war his property in Savannah being destroyed he removed to Richmond county and represented this county in the legislature from 1784 to 1789 inclusive as appears in the ... for these years. He subsequently removed from Richmond to Baldwin and died on Candler's hill three miles east of Milledgeville about 1815 having amassed a large estate. In personal appearance he was

[p. 43[4]]

fair complected heavy built and very corpulent weighing perhaps 280 pounds. He was affable and agreeable in his manners decidedly popular and had read much. He left four sons and one daughter who was the wife of Capt Ignatius Few of revolutionary fame. His sons were Henry Martin Joseph and Daniel and from them are sprung all who bear the name in Georgia at this time.

Very Truly yours

Daniel G. Candler

[p. 44]

Memos. to Danl. G. Candler, Apl. 4, 1871.

1st I infer yr. grandfather, Col. Wm. Candler, was born in Belfast, Ireland. Is this yr. understanding?

2d Was he a merchant or planter, or engaged in some other Employment? A letter of his among the Sumter papers loaned me by the family, indicated a very respectable education, writing a good, rapid, business chirography, leaving the impression with me that he was very likely a lawyer or merchant in his day.

3d. You seem to convey the idea that he did not settle in Richmond County till after the Revolution. From White's Statistics of Georgia we learn (page 499) that St.

Paul's Parish was in Richmond County; & from White's <u>Historical Collections</u> p. 604, we learn that he resided in that Parish in 1774. I only cite this fact to draw you out farther, if you possess any farther knowledge on this point.

4th Can you name any of the battles & skirmishes in which he was engaged, beyond the battles of King's Mountain, Fish Dam Ford, & Blackstocks, all in Oct. & Nov. 1780, mentioned

[p. 44[1]]

by <u>McCall</u> in his History of Georgia. I think he could not have been wounded in either of these battles; then where?

5th I should be glad if the dates of his birth & death could be arrived at, & his age. Is there any old family register, or any grave stone, giving dates & age, & any descendant residing near where he died, to whom you can refer me? The probate records of Baldwin County might give <u>about</u> the period of his death.

6th You may be able to refer me to other surviving grandchildren of Col. Candler — name & residence, who might give me some facts, even if isolated & disconnected.

7th When did yr. uncle <u>Henry Candler</u> die? If after 1832, he may have enjoyed the benefits of the Pension act of that year, & his declaration show both his & his father's services. If not, & he has surviving children, they may be able to specify <u>some</u> at least of his services, wh. wd. go to determine his father's.

8th Are yr. grandfathers' old papers preserved; if so, I wd. be glad to have their aid in my work.

Mention <u>Geo. W. Candler</u>, Buncombe Co. N. C. rep. in Leg. of that State in 1842. Wd. be glad to hear in reply, particularly to receive references before my departure on my Southern trip, as I may pass into Georgia, Alabama

&c, & might be able to see Some of them.

Send two parcels of pamphlets.

9th. Did yr. grandmother survive yr. grandfather, if so how long?

L. C. D.

[p. 45]

Gainesville, Hall County, Ga.
December 1st 1871

Hon Lyman C. Draper
Dear Sir

Your favor of April 4th did not reach me but that of the 20th December making further inquiry as to my grandfather William Candler is receivd and I take the earlyest oppertunity to answer your inquirey..

Since I last wrote to you I have obtained from the widow of My Cousin Ignacius A. Few a manuscript containing the History of our family by I A Few for the last hundred yeas which I think is authoritve. I A Few LL. D was a Col in the war of 1812 a fine Clacical scholar once an eminent Lawyer and ... at the time of his death president of Coney Collage his mother is a sister to my farther and his farther a Captan of Cavalry in the Revolutionary war. From the known Character of Dr Few I think the Manuscript is reliable. From it I gether The following facts.

Genl. Willim Candler was born of English parentage, in the City of Belfast Ireland about the year 1735 and at an early age emigrated to Virginia where he remained but a short time and went to North Carolina whare he was maried on the 12th day of May 1761 to Elizabeth Anthony Daughter of ... Anthony ... her mothers maiden name was ... Shortly after which time he emigrated and settled in Richmond County (New Colombia) Ga. His wife Elizabeth Anthony was born on the 21st of March 1746. They had the following Children Mary Henery Fathy William Charles Elizabeth John ...

[p. 45[1]]

Amelia Joseph Mark Anthony and Daniel who was my farther who maried Sarah Daughter of Samuel Slaughter of Baldwin County Ga. All Lived to be grown except Chares William and John Never maried Joseph Married but died without Issue Henry Married a Miss Oliver and had five daughters and only one son Who Married a Miss Reid was a Merchant in Macon Ga. of the firm of Smith Rogers & Candler he died leaving only one child Named Henery who now lives in Marion County Mis... & Maried a Miss Carr and raised a numerous family many of whome now live in Colombia County. Col William Candler was a man of strong will and well educated a Lawyer by profession but devoted his time mostly to farming. he had three farns one in Columbia Co (Fermed Richmond) one in Chatham and one in Baldwin two miles East of Milledgeville. The Journals of the house show that he represented Richmond County in the Legislature in 1784 & 1785. In 1785 he was appointed by the Govner Chief Justice. He had an interest in a Buisness house In Savannah and also in a Mill on his farm in Columbia (family ... at the time of his death he was said to be the largest land owner in the State his Estate at his death amounted to over $100,000.00. He died at his farm known as froot Hill in the fall of 1789 and was buried on it in Columbia County 4 miles East of Mount Carmel. His wife survived him and Married Capt William Disard Both of whome died and was buried on Sanders

[p. 45[2]]

Hill two miles East of Milledgeville (This is wnat decived me in my recolection of the place of grandfarthers death I said he was buried on Candlers hill that was Captain Disords & my grand Mothers burying place).

Most of the Information I have of his Millitay servis was derived from My uncle Majr Henry Candler who lived to an advanced age and died in October 1828 on his farm 12 miles West of Macon near the preasant Line of the H & N R. R. My uncle Henry Entered the service of the Colonies at the comencement of the war as Capt in his farthers Regiment and subsequently Rose to the rank of Major he ... me ... with betimes up ... and tho my memory ... distance of his ... yet I am not ... place or time ... my grandfarther was kindly ... was on the ... the Ga ... of the war. I think he ... any further military service ... to take Command of his Regiment ... his son ... of the R... while in ... of his farthers ... he was with ... His Regiment ... by a lively ... and in atempting to cut his way threw them he recived a severe ... across his head and ... his right arm. (The Bone between the Sholder ... in two and it never united

[p. 45[3]]

But hung loosely at his side still he was a good buismess man and ammassed a handsem fortune. You ask for Information as to the surviving relativs of William Candler. The only Ones that Left mail Issue was uncle Mark whose desendents Live mostly in Colombia Co. I Cannot give you there address. My farther Daniel Gandler died at the age of 34 years Leaving Five Sones & two Daughters The Oldest William died in Binnville parrish Louisanna a few years ago Leaving a Large family of children all of whome remain in Louisianna John Kingston Lives in Texes The next Samuel C Candler Lives in Villa Rica Carroll County Ga and has represented his County for many years in the Legislature of the State he is the farther of Milton A Candler (not D. G.) of decator Ga a senator in the preasent

Legislature. The next was E S Candler formely representative from Carroll County and 12 years Comptroler General of the state of Georgia. He died in Atlanata about two years ago Leaving no mail Issue except a small boy. I have been thuse voluminous in order to enable you to persue your enquiries further If you Desire. Nether my uncle Henery or the hers of my grandfarther ever applied for a pension they ware wealthy and did not need it. I am the youngest grandchild of Wm Candler a Lawyer and never aspired to any thing higher than the Judicial ermin Wishing you great sucess in your Laudable undertaking I remain

Yours &c

D. G Candler

[p. 46]

... 12th 1872

...

[p. 46[1]]

... Fruit Hill ... 1789 ... 1815 ... <u>Griff</u> ... never heard of ... Louisiana, <u>Claiborne</u> ...

[p. 46[2]]

...

[p. 46[3]]

From the Record of ... I ... She says her Grandfarther Mr Candler was Born in Belfast Ireland ... Virginia and from thence ... died in ...

[p. 46[4]]

The ... extending my ... and ... keeping up a kind of ... information on this head will you ... it will fill up ...

[p. 46a]
(typescript of pp. 46-46[4])

Ganesville Ga February 12th 1872

Hon. Lyman C. Draper
Dear Sir

Yours of 5th Instant has just come to hand and I reply by return mail. I have been Since the recipt of your last endeaving to procure all the authentic information I could on the subject of your inquiry. I have now before me two authentice Records one kept by Ignative A Few L.L.D. a son of my Farthers sister the other by Mrs Elizabeth A. Shiners oldest Daughter of My uncle Henry Candler. She died during the late war in her 84th year was a very inteligent Lady and well educated for her day. I have also Examined the Legislature records and fined that my grand farther represented Richmond County in the legislature several years. In my first Letter to you I stated that my grand farther died and was buried at his farm near Millidgevill. In this way Early recolections ware at fault. My grand farther had several Plantations one in Columbia Co this one I speak of at Millidgevill and a rice farm near Savonnah & also an interest in a Business house in Savnnah. My Grand farther died

on his farm in Columbia County Known as Fruit Hill in 1789 his widow afterwards married Capt. William Disard and movued to her farm 2 miles East of Milledgeville whare they both died Capt Discard in 1815 and My Grand Mother the year following. This probably is what made a false impression on my Infant Memory. I know nothing of Col McGriff never heard of him and know of no family of that name in the State. He must have moved soon after the war or died leaving no family. My uncle William Movued not to Missisipi But to Louisiana, Claiborne parish he was killed by a fall from a horse and Left only one son P. I. Candler who is now a practicing Physician in Arkansaw. I do not know his address I will now condense the Information that I gather from the family records of Dr Few. Col William Candler was Born in Belfast Ireland date not Known his farther was an English Merchant residnt at Belfast Col Candler Married Elizabeth Anthony Daughter of a James Idalim Emigrated to Virginia sometime before the Revolutionary war soon thare after

Emigrated to N. C. whare two of his first Children war Born. He then came to Georgia and settled in Richmond County (now Columbia) accumlated property rapidly had two Plantations and an Interest in a Mercantile house in Savanoh. At the opening of the Revolution took a disided part in favor of Collonies Raised a Redgment and equipted at his own expense (his Ridgement was called the Minuit men). His property was confiscated by the British government his negroes taken to Savanoh by the British army and his houses plundered and burned and his wife and children driven to a swamp for safty whare they Resided in a Camp for several Months. He was seriously wounded at Brier Breek in Ga towards the close of the war and never performed any further Military service. He represented Richmond County for several years after the war and died and was buried at his farm Known as fruit Hill in Columbia County 4 Miles East of Mt Carmel in 1789. His Widow subsequently married Cap William Discord and Removed to Candler hill farm 2 miles East of Milledbvill Whare they both Died Capt Discord in 1815 and his wife in 1816. This is Dr Fews letter Record in substance

From the Record of Miss Elizabeth A. Shinirs I colect the following facts. She says her Grand farther Mr Candler was

Born In Belfast Ireland and emigrated to Virginia and from thence to Ga. Before the Revolutionary was was an extensive planter and was a Copartiner in a trading house in Savanoh was a Col in the Revolution had his property Conficated and a reward offered for his scalp when the British armey evacuated Savanoh all his negroes Returned to the farms and went to work. He was twice wounded and in a Skimish with the Frees at Pine Bluff on the savonoh River and again at Brier Creek and was taken from the field after night By his wife and faithful body servant Peter (I recolect Peter he lived to be near 110 years old and was a Rampant whig to the day of his death). Her farther Major Henry Candler at 10 years old was sent back to his relatives In Ireland to be educated and at the opening of the war was recaled and entered the amey on his farthers staff perhaps as a volunteer ade and was severly wounded in Ga in a skimish with tory Ca ... and Raise to the Rank of Major. She farther states that her Grand farther William Candler died in the 68th year of his age

The Interest ...cited by this has sugested to me the importence of extending my investigation and writing and keeping up a kind of Family History. When you have Condensed your information in this head will you do me the favor to send me a Manuscript Copy of it. I shall be hopy at all times to Correspond with you on the subject and when your work is complete if desirable will accept the agency for the sale of the work in this state as it will fill up a vacuum in history of our state.

I fear you will not be able to Read this scrale all the Ink in this place has been reduced to ice during this protracted spell of cold weather.

Yours verry Turly

D. G. Candler

[p. 47]

Villa Rica Ga
Nov 29th 1871

L. C. Draper, Corr. Secy.
State Historical Society Wisconsin
Madison Wisconsin
Dear Sir

Your letter of 20th Inst. is to hand and noticed. I know but very little about Col. Wm. Candler of Revolutionary fame. I only know that when King George III isued his proclamation offering pardon to all who would return to their allegiance to the British government within a certain time with some exceptions that he was one of the exceptions. He was my father's great grand father, and came from Ireland and settled in South Carolina and in 1763 moved from there to Ga. to the place where Augusta Ga now is. Perhaps the Historical Society of Savannah Ga could give you some facts relative to him. I think Col. Mark A. Cooper of Cartersville Ga has a genealogical table of the Candler family for several generations back and would probably furnish you a copy of it were you to address

[p. 47[1]]

him. If the above facts which I hav given are worth any thing to you, you can use them.

Vey Respectfully,
William B. Candler

N. B. I reckon you could get "White's Statistics of Georgia" by writing to the State Librarian or Miss Phillips and crew (Bookselers) Atlanta Ga

W. B. C

[p. 48]

January 16th 1872

Mr. L. C. Draper

Sir yours of the ... duly ... I will ... Wm Candler ... recollections ... been ... Combined in ... will be ... satisfactory.

... Wm. Candler ... recollect of his Military Service and lived in Columbia County ... old letters. Copies in ... high ...faced

[p. 48^1]

...

... Col. Henry Candler the Son ... Col ... from him ... Revolutionary ... family and ... and ... father, ... and prominent Mason.

[p. 48^2]

... the widow of ... with this ... wishes for your success in such a noble undertaking, ... able. Sincerely ... most respectfully ...

M... Sanders

... Macon Ga ... Co. Gray

Sanders

[p. 49]

Col. Wm. Candler, Maj. Benjn. Few.

Ganesville Ga May 14th 1878

Lyman C Draper Esqr.

Dear Sir,

Your of the 10th Instant came to hand yesterday and found me still in life and in good health for one of my age I was glad to here from you again and Especilly to learn that you had not yet Completed your work on Genl Sumpter as it will afford me am opportunity of correcting several errors that I made in our Correspondence in regard to my grandfarther Col Wm. Candler. I spoke then from reminicens and Impressins made on My mind when a verry small child. I have since been engaged in writing up a genl family record for the satisfaction of my children and grandchildren I visited Louisanna to confer with my only surviving brother John H... Candler who is the only suirviving brother that I have and is 11 years older then myself and consequently can recolect our family history much better. I have obtained valuable information from the records is the ... as to his public service after the war I have also ... from numbers of the family records which shows the dates of his birth death and mariage &c. I will imbody this information as soon as I can find time and send it to you I think you will find it correct. But it is two voluminous to be communicated in this letter. You enquire concerning Majr Benjamin Few. I gave you all the information embraced in Col Fews manuscript refered to H... William Few, his grandfarther died in the year 1793 in Columbia County, Ga; and was buried at the then residince of his eldest son Benjamin Few leaving the following children (to wit: 1 Benjamin

[p. 49[1]]

who commanded a redgiment of Jartigen Whiggs during the ware of the Revolution and fought many a battle. He died on the Tombigbee river in 1805. (He go... to ...) his Uncle James Few who was the first victim of the ware having been put to death by the Tories in North Carolina. Next he mentions William Few* who was Liutenant Colonel of the ridgement commanded by his Bro. Benjn. Subsequently was Judge of the Superior Court in Ga. Delegate from that state in the Convention which formed the constitution of the united States and for many years senator in Congress he was born in June 1747 and died in the City of New York in the summer of 1828. Dr. Few then mentions his farther Igntius Few Who mareed the Daughter of Col Wm. Candler he was borne on the 20th of August 1750 he was a Capt of Dragoons in the Continental army fought many battles was for 7 month a prisoner in Augusta while the British held that post and retired at the close of the ware with the rank of Major He died at his residence in Columbia County Ga on the 18th Febrary 1810. He then mention the daughters of the family which it is not necary here to mention.

I will be pleased to continue this correspondence with you and would like to have a few copies of the work when it appears at subscription prices.

Very truly yours &c.

Daniel G. Candler

*Memo. by LCD: As Col. Wm. Few was born in 1748, probably Maj. Benjn. was born about 1744, hence about 61 when he died. Wm. descended from Wm. Ffew, a Wm. Penn emigrant, & the younger Wm. born in 1748, was a native of Baltimore Co. Md., & his parents removed in 1758 to Orange Co. N. C. where Wm. recd. a good education, & inferentially Benjamin also.

[p. 50]

Gainesville Ga May 23rd 1878

Lyman C. Draper Esq

Dear Sir: yours dated May 20th recved by last nights mail & have againe refered to to Dr. Fews manuscript and find that he, Benjn Few died on Tombigbee river, Ala in 1805, and belive that this is strictly correct as Dr Few certainly knew and would not have mistaken it. you ask the address of My brother; it is John H Candler Mount Lebanon, Binnville Parish, La. I think, however, he will not be able to give you the information you desire as he was born in 1801 and was only 4 or 5 years old when Majr <u>Benjn Few</u> died. As reguards the corrections of my statements in reguard to <u>Col Wm. Candler</u> I have received [a MS.] from an old gentleman in Virginia who spent a few months here last summer by the name of Evans who is Connected with the <u>Candler</u> family by marriage. This MS. bears date in 1785 and says that The farther of <u>Col William Candler</u> emigrated from Belfast Ireland with his family in or about 1710. His two sones <u>William</u> and <u>Zachariah</u> ware born in Ireland <u>William</u> was perhaps Born in 1738. The two sones ware sent back to Belfast and recived there a Clasical Education. On the compleation of there education

[p. 50[1]]

They returned to there farthers residence in Prince Edward Co virginia at the foot of a small hill or mountain now known as <u>Candler's</u> mountain There farther farmed and rane a country store. In 1761 <u>Col. William Candler</u> was maried to <u>Elizabeth Anthony, daughter</u> of <u>Mark Anthony</u> whose Farther was a Genoesee station; She was born in virginia on the 21st of march 1746. Soon after his marrige in 1762, <u>William</u> and <u>Zach Candler</u> emigrated to Hawood County N. C. Where the first four children of <u>Wm. Candler</u> were born (to witt) <u>Mary, Henry, John</u> & <u>Ophalley</u>. He then emigrated to Richmond County, Ga in or near Augusta Whare he remained engaged in farming and merchandizing untill the commencement of the Revolutionary war. When he recived from the Continental Congress a Commision of Col and was assigned to <u>Sumpter's</u> brigade, in which capacity he served till The Close of the war. He was never seriously wounded as stated by me from family tradion. It was my step Grand farther, <u>Capt William Disert</u> who maried my grand mother after My grand farther's death, and who was a Capt. in grand farthers regiment. The service which he performed was mostly detached services on the Georgia side of the river. He took part in the fights at Kings mountane, Blackstocks farm, Bryer Creek and many other battles and skirmishes mostly with the Tories to whome he was said to be a Terrore. During the war he was outlawed

[p. 50[2]]
by the British athorties together with 151 others prominent whigs provided they did not appear and take the prescribed oath in a given time. He failed to comply and while the british held savnah They sent a force and plundered and burned his houses and fences and caried off his negroes 43 in number and kept them there untill they evacuted the place, when the negroes being turned loose all come back to there master except two who had died while captives (For act of confisction see Whites Histrical Colections extracts from Colonial record) I see from the parish record in Augusta that he took the contract to build the first Baptist church that was ever built in Augusta After the close of the war he engaged in farming and merchantdizing and speculating in head-right lands in Georgia and became wealthy. It appers farm the Jornals of the Legislature of Ga, that he was a member of the legislature from Richmond County, and afterwords from Columbia County untill the day of his death which took place in September 1789. He was baried on his farm known as fruit Hill 4 miles east of Mount Carmel church in Columbia County Ga I have recently visited his grave a Granate granite head stone marks his grave with no inscription save his name Col. Wm. Candler died September, 1789. The day of the month is defaced and is not legible. His wife survived him and maried Capt William Disert, who was a captain in my Grandfarthers redgiment They settled on a farm bequeathed to her by her

first husband now known as Candlers hill 2 miles east of Milledgeville they both died and were buried there, marble Slab marks the grave of my grand mother

[p. 50[3]]

and a granate head-stone that of my step-grand farther with no inscription except the name Capt Wm. Disert. I was also mistaken in my statement that my uncle Henery Candler entered the armey as an offcer. I learn from my older brother and uncle Henry Candlers oldest Daughter, Mrs Elizabeth A. Shiners, who died in Sparta Ga recently that uncle Henery entered the service at the Comencement of the war as a kind of courier for his farther at the age of 12 years. When he was only 16 years old while engaged in this kind of service he was persued by a party of British Dragoons and attenting to escape ... was overtaken and so unmerciefully hacked up with a saber that he was left for dead but was taken up by his mother and got well but was unable to do any sevice during the remainder of the war. The fact that shortly after the war he was elected served as major of militia in Columbia Co Ga led me into the error as he was called by I have seen the Scares was when a boy talk about him a Great deal. Zach. Candler remained in North Carolina and is the progenitor of all the North Carolina Candlers. He belonged to the Loyalist during the war tho' did not fight. This so insensed my grand farther that they never spoke to each other afterwards and there desendents even now refuse to fraternize. I am certain that with these corrections the information I have given you is Correct for I have gone to the bottom with the investigation to satisfy myself and to perfect my family record.

Yours truly

Daniel G. Candler

[p. 51]

Gainesville Ga June 1st 1878

Lyman C. Draper Esqr.

Dear Sir yours of the 26th ult recevd several days ago press of buisness has prevented an early reply. Since the date of my last I have recived your Complyment of the ... Histrical Colections Catalogue &c And have read your colection with a great deal of pleasure and find it verry interesting. You are certainly doing a great work for your state as well as for the entire to this Country. But in view of the exertions now being made to preserve the history of our country I ...itiated on account of my own ... state. The ... state of the ... that she has scarcely any history except a vol of statistics and meager extracts from the colonial records. And that many battles (or rather skirmishes) between the Whigs and tories fought in her am sure he never found a place in her writen History. On reference to the Few MS I find that you are correct in the orthography of Capt. Dysart's name. You are also correct in your conjecture as to the year of my birth. I was born February 22nd 1812 and am the youngest child of Daniel Candler Who was the youngest of the children of Col. William Candler. I know nothing that would be ... about Capt. McCoy for whome you enquire I have heared my grandfarther, Samuel Slaughter (mothers farther) Speake of a ...are ... Scotchman of that name, who had a verry saniary method of disposeing of Tories that had the misfortune to fall into his hands. He commanded what was called minute men, a kind of home-guards who worked on their farms a portion of the time and fought in ...

[p. 51[1]]

of emmergency. This may have been the man for whome you enquire. As to the time at which my great grandfarther removed from Ireland to virginia I have it in his family history about the year 1740. This is only Conjectural and deduced from the fact that Mrs Elizabeth Shiners, uncle Henry Candler's oldest Daughter who died in Sparta Ga in the 87th year of her age, She died about 4 years ago And who was a woman of remarkable intelect and retained her memory to the time of her death, That she had once had in her posesion the family record of her grand farther William Candler as well as a heavy gold ring with the name Wm. Candler inscribed on it and some other relicts I sa the relicts but the family record She said had been carried off by some of the family many years ago. She was certain that her Grandfarther was maried to Elizabeth Anthony in 1761 and that he was in his 25th year when maried That she said was the ... this would make his birth year 1738 and she stated that this mariage took place soon after his return from Ireland whare he had been sent to finish his education. The rec... says he was born in Ireland and educated thare. The manuscript Shown me last summer by Mr J E Levins an old gentleman who spent a portion of last Summer here and who was a desendent of the Anthony family Contaned the Births Mariages and deaths of that family for several generations back, and farm which I was permited to take notes, Says that Elizabeth Anthony was maried in Janary 1761 to a man by the name of Wm. Candler who was by Birth and education an Irishman whos. parents emigrated from the vicinity of Belfast and settled in Prince Edward County va. This evidence settles these facts 1st That he was an Irishman by birth and Education. 2d That his farther emigrated at some time after his birth to Prince Edward County Va The place where he settled is still known as Candler's Hill (by some as Candlers Mountain) 3rd That in 1761 He was maried to Elizabeth Anthony ...

[p. 51[2]]
He and his widow ware ... he was dead and his widow maried before ... it was hoped ... revolutionary soldiers and I know that Her Husband ... applyed for a pension for his Revolutionary service. Verry few ... men would accept it But ... who actually needed it applyed for it. On the ... his having been under the command of Sumter I have no ... only ... McCall's story and recolections of statements by uncle Henry Candler ... Samuel Slaughter (was since in the same Regement ... who served in the Revolutionary ... these persons was that it ... by Wm. ... ... subject ... to the orders of Genl Sumter. They ware kept most of the time on the lines, till ... as a kind of local Gaoler to keep down the depredations from tories ... with ... who served with him ... his ...fought at Kings mountain Blackstocks, ... and many other places ... so called ... Few ... said to be ... with the ... mission after ... of a ... The fight at ... is ... he was ... into ... enemy ... massed his men and charged ... into his way ... and with st... used to go to ... that is ... to have whipped ... by ... that the statements were ... is ... whare history ... is ... to ... written ... to

[p. 51[3]]
lead us to correct conclusions.

With much respect I remain yours

D. G. Candler

[p. 52]

Hastings on Hudson River
Oct 29, 1873

Lyman C Draper Esqr
Dear Sir

I write at my mothers request to thank you for your valuable work in Wisconcin & to answer your enquiries as to Major Ben: Few. Your note would have answered more promptly, but my Mother is now at her city residence, & her country house was unoccupied so that I had some difficulty in finding the memoirs of my grandfather, Col Wm. Few.

P. S. I should judge from my grandfathers memoir that Benjamin Few was probably born in North Carolina on the banks of the river Eno Orange County, as his father was residing there about that time. W.F.C.

[p. 52[1]]
It was in Dec 1778 after the British had defeated Genl Howe & taken possession of Savannah. The plundering parties of the Enemy ranged through the greatest part of the country without opposition. The whole force of the State then Consisted of the Militia of the 3 upper counties which did not in the whole exceed 500 men. My brother commanded the malitia of Richmond county & determined to check the progress of those parties. He raised about 200 men & was joined by Col. Twiggs with about 50 or 60. They advanced towards Savannah, about 30 miles below Augusta, & erected the American standard & formed their Camp.

[p. 52[2]]
"The Legislature Convened in Savannah under the new Constitution, And their first act was to appoint a Governor & 16 executive councillors. I was chosen a member of that Council.

We had not yet felt the effect of war nor did we apprehend danger until we were alarmed at the approach of Genl. Provost with the British Army from East Florida. he had passed Sunbury & had penetrated within 40 miles of Savannah, spreading terror & devastation. Every person was called to arms, and as many volunteers as could be enrolled were required to immediately advance & meet the Enemy. With those volunteers I marched in full expectation of coming to action but we were most agreeably disappointed, for the Enemy retreated before we came within ten miles of him. This invasion from East Florida roused the indignation of the Georgians, & they resolved on retaliation. A plan was formed for attacking St. Augustine which was the Capitol of East Florada. In the Spring of 1778 the Military force of the State was Collected which Consisted of

[p. 52[3]]
militia and 6 or 800 Continental troops which were Commanded by Genl Howe. The malitia was Commanded by Gov. Houstoun. This force was supposed to be sufficient for the conquest of East Florida. But the whole was defeated, not by the sword of the Enemy, but by the dissention of the Govr. & General. They Contended which should have the Command until the Season for military operations was so far advanced, the hot weather commenced and the fever raged in their camp And destroyed more than a general action. A retreat became necessary to save the remainder of the troops of which near one half had been destroyed, or dispersed without seeing the face of an enemy.

Thus terminated an expedition foolishly planned & worse executed. We had neither stores of provisions, munitions of war, nor money in the Treasury."

[p. 52[4]]

Some years before his death he wrote a memoir which has never been published & & in fact was only intended for his family. This memoir is the only source which she thought could contain any answer to your enquiries for she herself does not find that she has any recollection sufficiently accurate to be of any use to you. The memoir is long but I can only find one referrence to his brother

[p. 52[5]]
in Burk county & detached parties of cavalry to intercept the enemy, &c &c." Then follow an account a surprise by the enemy & a repulse, but no special mention of Major Benjamin Few. My Grandfather was subsequently appointed Leiut Col.; & in 1780 he was appointed a member of Congress, &, in May of that year set out for Philadelphia, so that he was not in way of meeting his brother & in fact does not mention him. My mother desires me to express her regret in not being able to give you any information residing, as she did at the north, she was never thrown in company with her uncle.

Very Sincerely
W. F. Christie

[p. 53]

Hastings on Hudson
Dec 3d

L. C. Draper Esqr.
Dear Sir,

My mother is in the city so I have not seen her in regard to your questions but she told me that she remembered nothing Certain about Maj. Ben Few. On examining the memoir I think Major Ben. Few as older than my grandfather.

As regards the Expedition to Florida the memoir Contains the following notice. The date of the expedition he fixes as you will see in 1778, but it may be an error as he mentions his removal to Georgia in the Autumn of 1776. at that time he was elected a member of the Convention which formed the Constitution of the State he then Continues,

[p. 53[1]]

I find the following mention of Col. Williamson. The British took possession of the State of Georgia & had their head quarters at Augusta.

"I collected a few men & crossed the Savanah river & joined Genl. Williamson who commanded the malitia of So.Carolina & had embodied about 1500 men on the bank of the river opposite to Augusta within view of the enemy". The memoir then mentions the retreat of British the result of the Movements of Genl. Lincoln who Commanded the Continental Army in South Carolina, & his own services when in a volunteer detachment of 200 horsemen employed to pursue & harass the Enemy on his March he does not however mention Genl. Williamson again. I find no mention of Coll. Clark & Candler. I believe I have answered all your questions it will give me pleasure to be of service to you in any way in my power.

Truly y
W. F. Christie

[p. 54]

"Few Family. Where can I find out any thing about the family of Few, an ancient Norman family, descended from the Count de Feu? Their habitat in the country was the Isle of Goty, where there is a book about them. They have a brazier ... with a punning Motto, Feu "sert et sauve".

H. Pugh"

Notes & Queries, Apl. 22d 1882

Col. Benjn. Few.

Augusta Georgia ... 22 1873

... 17 my ... but ... office ... Benj. Few was a ... an uncle of my mother, removed from Ga. to the Black Warrior country (now in Alabama) beyond ... New, but ... I am unable to say. He left Ga. I suppose about the beginning of this Century. I believe ... he was born in Hillsborough N. C. the date I do not know, but I think it was between 1740 & 1750. I think he was engaged in the battle of Beechford some 30 Mile South of this place. I am also very sure that he was with Gates and was Captured & made a prisoner, but made his escape. I think he was with Cinch in an un...ed attack on

[p. 54[1]]

t... place, & was an active partisan ... doubtless ... on the ... left two sons. Both married. Wm. the elder left a son & daughter. The daughter never married; the son married and I believe left but one child ... whatever became of her I know not. The younger son Thos. left several children. His boys died without issue. He had two daughters living in this County. I have not seen them for two or three months. When I do, I will make enquiry about their Grandfather, though I presume they would have no information, as Benj. Few left some years before they were born. their father left for Alabama many years ... were just ... know little of my kindred ... Democratic institutions rather ... of one's ancestors

[p. 54[2]]

... you left ... may find a Confirmation of ... the time of Judge Johnson on ... you ...

Respectfully,

I. P. Garvin

[p. 55]
(illegible)

[p. 56]
Madison, Geo. Oct 6, 1875.
L. C. Draper
Dear Sir:

Yours of 24th of June to hand & notice what you say. I have made every effort to find out for you. There was a man by that name, Maj. Ben. Few; but can't find out where he moved to, & where he died. I can't give you any information concerning him.

Their lives one Wm. A. Few in California. If he can't give you the information you wish, I do not know who can. His address: Wm. A. Few. Jackson, Amador Co: California.

Yours &c

I. C. Few, Sr.

[p. 56[1]]
Memo.

See Letters of Geo. G. McWhorter of Oct. 1873 & May 1878, & also D. G. Chandler's of May, 1878, showing that Maj. Few settled in the region of Claiborne, Monroe County, Alabama, early in this century & died there in 1805.

See also note I appended to Mr. Candler's letter above, showing that Maj. Few was a native of Baltimore Co. Md. & born in or abt. 1744, his parents removing to Orange Co., N. C., in 1758, where Benjamin wad educated. This inferential from date in his brother Col. Wm. Few's memoirs. L. C. D.

Majr. Few in service in 1780, summer or autumn: Johnson's Traditions, 531.

[p. 57]

Notes from Loskiel's Hist. of the Missions.

The first mission to N. A. by the Moravian Brethren was in 1735. It was to the State of Georgia. It prospered but the Brethren at length refusing to bear arms when called on by the civil authority & altercations arose which caused them to leave that state & go to Pennsylvania. A number of the Brethren had gone there about the same time that those just mentioned went to Georgia. Count Linzindorf was the Patron & director of these early operations.

Pages 1-10

They began to settle & build in Bethlehem in 1740 Nazareth was owned by Mr. Whitfield who began to build a house for the education of Negro children before 1740. It was afterwards sold to the Brethren. First Indian Church, established at P. 16. The home... 1740. It was among the Mahican Indians, not far from Poughepsia on the borders of Connecticut. They were obliged to leave that & at length their Indian Converts on account of their being charged with alliance with the French. Their converts were about ...00 in No. These were Shawanese on the Deleware.

[p. 57[1]]

The principal Missions among the N. Amer. Indians have been established by the the Society of United Brethen, Unitas Fratrum, Commonly termed Moravian Brethren. As early as 1734, such of the Brethren resided in the village of Berthelsdorf in the Marquasite of Upper Lusatea set out for America under the superintendence & direction of Count Linzendorf. They landed in Pennsylvania but according to their Original design proceeded to Georgia. Meeting with insuperable difficulties in that quarter they returned to Pens...van... in 1740. These indefatigable ... with others that arrived soon after after ... Commenced the work of

Christian instruction among the Indians of Pemnsilvia New Jersey New York & Connecticu. Bethlem on the river Lehigh in Pennsia was ... & has contin. ever since their principal town. After susta... great persecution and injury during the wars that preceeded the Cession of Canada to Great Brittain the Missionaries with their flock consisting chiefly of Delewares & Mahicans, made a new settlement, termed Gnadenshutten higher up the Susquhannah than any previous one. From this settlement in 1767, a missionary was detached to some Deleware towns on the Allegheny river. Meeting with great opposition here in 1767, with 6 converted families they moved farther down the river & in the year following they ascend Big Beaver on the eastern

[p. 57[2]]
Confine of this State & made a settlement which they termed Friedenstad or Town of Peace. The Mission prospered better here but in 1772 the ... missionary Zeisberger, with 5 conv familes made a visit to the Muskingum. They made a settlement at a place which they named Schoenbrun or Beautiful Spring, which was the begiming of their Mission in this State. In the Meantime the congregations on the Susquehanna Consisting of 140 persons from the Sale, by the Iroquois of the land on which they lived, determined to emigrate, and on the 11 June 1772 they set out for the Muskingum. Upon reaching that river they Choose a place about 10 miles below Schoenbrun to which they gave the name of Gnadenhutten or Tents of Grace. In 1773 the remainder of the Congregation at Beaver Creek emigrated to Schoenbrun, which together with Gnadenhutten Contained all the converts of the Society then alive. The former place was inhabited Chiefly by Delawars & the latter principally by Mahikans. At these places, under the direction of the Missionary Zeisberger, Hoeckenweilder,

Rothe, & Schmeck the Congregat. began to flourish much.

Their properity was not however long ...ded. The war between G. B. & her Col... the Missionaries to a great dilemma. They had as servants of God to remain neutral: the Cols. did not require them to take part in

[p. 57[3]]

in the Contests but G. B. whose policy was to enlist the Indians generally on her side, inflamed the minds of those nations which surrounded the Congregations & until they seriously required the latter to join in the Contest. In 1776 a part of the Congregation under the direction of Z & H. left Shonb. to form a third settlemt lower down on the Musk. which was termed Lichtenau. The believing Indians at this time being upwards of 400 in number, living in 3 Contgs. Setlemts., had const... defying intercourse & not with... their external troubles, had ... much internal prosperity. A reading & Spelling book Compiled by Z. in the Del Lang. was introduced into their schools & gave great pleasure to the schollars. The Delewares had formerly resolved to remain & neutral as and the other Indian tribes & the English ascribed that ... to the infl. of the Miss. a Sheme was concerted to convey the latter to Detroit. At length in 1778 drawn into the Engl. Ints. but as the Missionas. remaind firm the scheme of carryg. them to detroit was not abandond. In 1780 however the Mission enjoyed peace & rest, but it was of short duration for in 1787 a party of Inds. with Engls. Col. & an Eng. Captn. arrived. They commtd. many outrages & at length compd. the whole congregations with the superts. to set out for Detroit. The savages driving them forward like a herd of cattle. The savages Deserted them at upper Sandusky but but not long after a message arrived from the gov. at Dett. reqg. the ... that place. None of the ... out of ... repaired thither. P. 165 left off.

[p. 57[4]]
In their several intervews with the Governor they fortunately succeeded in convincing him of their innocence and of the perfect neutrality they had observed derring the war the rasult of this Conviction in the governor was the performance of Several acts of hospitality and permission to return to their Congregation which they immediately did. The state of the cong. was such however as to detract very much from the joy they felt upon returning. The scarcty of food was such as to constitue a real famine, which threatening destruction to the whole mission induced a large number to return to the M. for the purpose of bringing away the crops of corn that were left growing when they were driven from that region. During thair stay at their late habitations they ware all murderated by a party of lawless Americans. But the deleberate massacre of 96 Most harmless men women & children ... though the greatest was not the only evil that befel this devoted people during this year. Immideatly after the Misss. were discrarged by the Govr. the enemies of the Mission renewed their Callumnies & the consequence was that the ... Miss. & their famils. were obliged ... to repair to detroit. The Govr. persud. them to remain in Detr. or to return to Bethlm. but with his consent the made a settlement in 1782 on the River Huron abt. 30 miles above detroit. Thither the Indian of the Congregation which after the departure of the Missonaries had become very much dispersed repaired, the settlement began to flourish & the congregn. grady. increased till 1784 when they Chippeways on whose land they were requird then moved the missonaries decided on a migration

[p. 57[5]]
to the S. side of lake Erie which was accompd. in 1786. They fixed on a spot several days journey up the Cayahogo

river & immedtly. commenced its improvement. From the society at Bethlem, from the Congress of the U. S. & from several private characters they recieved considerable assistance. Their wish was to return to the Muskingum but the war at that time Carrying on between the Ind. & the U. S. renderd such a measure improper & the belligerent tribes reqrd. them to remove from the Coyahoga the established themselves in May 1787 at the Mouth of the small river Huron & mamed the place New Salem.

[p. 57[6]]

When we review the zeal disinterestedness, talent industry & piety of the numerous Missionaries employed for so many years in this work of ... reformation, we regret but their labours not ...ized that were not more successful, we are rather astonished that they should have made so many converts than that they did not make more. An unconquerable passion for military glory, attachment to the life of the hunter, pride, a spirit of personal independence, & blind attachment to the ... & superstition of their forefathers constituted a phalanx of opposition which we could expect even Christian ... & perseverance but partially to overcome.

[p. 57[7]]

Loskiel's
Histy. of the Missns.
Extract.

[p. 58]

Madison, Wisn. Jan. 21st, 1870.

Dr. John A. Hill
My Dear Sir:

I have already written you once, or twice, relative to your grandfather, Col. Wm. Hill, of the Revolution. Your brother Gen. D. H. Hill, has kindly communicated to me such facts as he knew, & has referred me to various sources of information; but he has not been able to inform of the date of yr. grand-father's death, & age.

If you can inform me of these data, I shall

[p. 58[1]]

feel exceedingly thankful for them, & doubly so for any additional facts about your grandfather's life & services.

If you have not the dates I seek of your grandfather's death & age, still you may be able to approach pretty nearly to these; if so, state your impressions.

Whenever I write to any one in Mississippi, I am reminded of my residence at Pontotoc, in your State, thirty years ago, editing a Democratic paper there, &, so

[p. 58[2]]

it is, I still find my associations with the conservative Democracy of the country. The Hon. John F. H. Claiborne, Sheldsboro, Miss, is the only one of the old set of prominent Mississippians (I might perhaps add Hon. Jacob Thompson, with whom I was very slightly acquainted) whose friendship I still retain, & occasionally receive a warm-hearted, genial letter from him. Pardon this digression.

Very sincerely yours,
Lyman C. Draper.

P. S. Can you refer to any of yr. cousins who might

[p. 58[3]]
be able to give me any facts or traditions about your grandfather Col. Hill?

Pray can you give me any facts about yr. grandfather Ths. Cabeen, dates of birth & death & incidents & services of the Revolution?

L. C. D.

[p. 59]

Alabama.
Steggins MSS.
Driesbach Letters.

Baldwin Co. Ala.
July 13th 1874

Hon Lyman Draper
Dear Sir,

I sent you some 30 pages manuscript, written by myself, in regard to the early history of Ala. Did you receive it. I sent it to Mobile, to be sent from there by express. I was in error, in regard to John Weatherfords education, it was very limited. In other respects he was, as I stated him to be. Please make the correction. Did you receive the photograph of Chas. Weatherford, sent by Dr. Moore.

Respectfully,
I. D. Dreisbach

Dr Thoms recd. the books, and said he write to you in a short time.

[p. 60]

Baldwin Co. Ala. May 3d 1874

Mr. Lyman C. Draper
Dear sir,

Your letters with books &c. came to hand a few days since. I have had several copies of Gen Woodwards Reminiscences of Ala, but they have been carried off and I do not know where to obtain one at present. I may possibly be able to procure a copy in Montgomery when I go there in November next, if so I will express it to you. The letters written to me by Gen Woodward, have passed out of my hands. I may possibly send you a copy at some future time.

I have not had time to read the books & pamphlets you were kind enough to send me, but in hastily glancing over the pages of "Wisconsin Historical Collections" and some of the pamphlets I see that Wisconsin was tainted in a preeminent degree with that fanatical spirit which has ever pervaded the political an social atmosphere of the New England states, And which was the first and great cause of the of the terrible and bloody conflict which has brought ruin and sorrow to almost every household of this once

[p. 60[1]]

prosperous and beautiful land of flowers, but now the most helpless and Radical cussed country on Gods green earth. I would tread softly on the ashes of the dead, but must say (with becoming respect) that where prominent men holding the political opinions and doctrines which were entertained by Hon Charles Durkee Gov L. P. Harvey & many other prominent men of your state, who moulded and fashioned the political opinions of Wisconsin, we who live here in the south, and were its former slave holders, can very easily understand how this unnatural and patricidal war was precipitated upon us. In contreadistinction to these sectional feelings and opinions, it is refreshing to listen to the beautiful, profound, eloquent, brave and patriotic words and sentences of such gentlemen as Paul A. Chadbourne, as expressed in his Annual Address before the Wisconsin State

Historical Society, in 1868. And the classical and graceful Annual address of the Hon Anthony Van Wyck in 1867. But even him, (A. V. W), with all his classic lore and charming eloquence, must throw a "tub to the whale", and give the poor

[p. 60²]

prostrate south a kick, by his "prison pens of the South." The people of the South fought for the right, and therir native land, and it is idle and absurd to say that the South commenced the war, for it is patent to all intelligent minds, that, had there never been any abolitionists, there never would have been any secessionists. But pardon me, for my digressions. I cannot but feel warmly when this subject is brought to my mind. Fraternal feeling for those people again, never, never, never again with this generation.

I may at some future date write something, in relation to the Indians and early settlers of this country. My family, being connected by ties of consanguinity and Marriage with most of the prominent Indians, and half breeds of the Creek Nation. My wifes father was a nephew of Alex McGilvery, and half brother of William Weatherford.

I have the honor to be,
Very Respectfully,
Your obt. svnt.
I. D. Dreisbach

[p. 61]

Mr Lyman C. Draper,
Dear Sir,

If the express Charges are paid in Mobile, you can remit them to C. H. Dreisbach, Mobile.

Respectfully,

I. D. Dreisbach

July, 1874.

I will send "Reminiscences of Ala" if I can procure a copy.

[p. 62[1]]

Baldwin Co. Ala., July, 1874

Lyman C. Draper, Esqr.
Madison Wisconsin
Dear Sir,

In compliance with your request, I give you a few historical facts in regard to the early settlers and pioneers of Alabama. I have gathered My information on this subject from personal intercourse with some of the parties, and from family papers and other old musty records of the dim past, which I find amongst my father in laws (David Tates) papers, and particularly many incidents in the history of Alexr. McGilvery, and Wm. Weatherford, they both being relations of my wife, McGilvery being the uncle of my wifes father and Weatherford being his (Tates) half brother, Tates & Weatherfords mother being a sister of McGilverys. Lauchlin McGilvery (the father of Alex McGilvery was descended from a Scotch Nobleman. he came to Savanna Georgia, sometime in the early part of the seventeenth century; from there he went to the Creek Nation, then in the uper part of this State; there he took for a wife a full blooded Indian woman of the Tuskegee, or Wind family.

[p. 62[2]]

2

The Wind family being the most aristocratic in the Creek, or Muscogee Nation. He had five children by this wife, named as follows Alexr., Sehoy, Jennie, Elizabeth, and Sophia. Alexr. was the General Alexr. McGilvery mentioned in Pickets History of Alabama, and was no doubt one of the most remarkable men that this state has ever produced, White or Red. When he visited Genl. Washington (during Washingtons Presidential term,) he took with him his son and my wifes father, who were then boys about ten and fourteen years of age. He left them there at school under the eye of Washington, who took charge of them and boarded them in his own family. They remained there five years, and were then sent to Scotland to school, where they remained two years, when young McGilvery died. My father in law then returned and spent a portion of his time in the Creek Nation, when he removed to Baldwin County in this State, where he remained until he died in 1829. Sehoy, the eldest of McGilverys sisters, Maried Col John Tate, who was at that time acting as agent for the British Goverment. At the commencement of the Revolution

[p. 62[3]]

3

Tate raise a large body of Indians (about 1500) and went to Savanna, or started there, when he became deranged, and was carried back to the Nation, where he died. By his marriage with Sehoy, he had but one child named David, who was the father of my wife, and of Elouisa Tate, who married Col George Tunstall of Virginia, by whom he had seven children, the eldest one was named Thos. Tate Tunstall, who was U. S. Consul at Cadiz in Spain, when the war broke out in 1861. He was arrested by order of the U S Goverment, for sympathising with The Lost Cause, and carried to Boston in chaines. He was released from Fort Warren, and again arrested in Washington City, as a spy, but not being able to convict him as such he was released on conditions that he would be sent to Europe, there to remain until after the close of the war. He was sent over on a

Goverment man of war, where he remained until 1866. His father had two brothers who ocupied high social positions, one being a physician of high standing, and the other was Secretary of State during Bagbys term as Governor of Ala. The Doctor was the father of the wife of U. S. Senator C. C. Clay of Ala. She was one of the most popular

[p. 62[4]]

and fascinating ladies who visited Washington City. She is still the Idol of her family, as well as of a large circle of friends and admirers. David Tate had two other daughters, one of whom is dead, and the other one in Texas. Genl Alex McGilvery has no children living, he had three, Alexr., Margaret and Elizabeth; Alexr. died in Scotland, as I mentioned before. Gen McGilverys wife was a full blood, of Tuskegee town of Indians. After the death of John Tate, his wife Sehoy Tate married Charles Weatherford (an Englisman) by whom she had six children, named as follows, William, John, Elizabeth, Major, Mary, and Rosannah, who was the youngest, and is still living. William Weatherford (who was the terrible hero of Fort Mims, and the Hotspur of the Creek Indians) was born at Talisee, in the uper part of this State, about the year 1774. He was reared to manhood in his native forest, with the book of Nature spread out before him, which was his only teacher, or guide. He was well skilled in all the arts of hunting and woodscraft, as well as the rude art of war, as practiced by his people. Nature appeared to have been lavish of her favors in the physical adornment of his person, for he was said to have been in

[p. 62[5]]

5

form, a perfect man, with all the physical graces which Nature can bestow. He was 6 feet and 2 inches in hight, and weighed about 175 lbs, with a form of perfect mould, with the bearing and air of a Knight of the olden times. In activity and muscular power he had no peer amongst his people, and as he stood forth in his pride of manhood he looked as though he was born to command, "and that there was none to dispute his sway". Though fierce and terrible in battle, he was gentle and kind as a lady to the weak and helpless, and generous and liberal to all when Nature had its sway. And it was this noble generosity of his nature which came very near being the cause of his loseing his life at the massacre of Fort Mimes in this county, during the war of twelve and fourteen. The night bebore the attack on the fort, he camped with his 600 warriors near where I am now living. He made them a talk and proposed to them, that in the event they took the fort, not to kill the women and children, said that they had come to fight warriors, and not squaws. The warriors accused him of having a "forked tongue and white heart", told him that he wanted to spare

[p. 62[6]]

6

his relations (several of whom were in the fort,) and there was several attempts made during the night to assassinate him. He led them on and attacked the fort the next day, and as soon as the Indians had fired the roofs of some of the houses in the fort, and commenced cutting down the pickets, he (Weatherford) rode off and went to his half brothers (David Tates) plantation and took all the slaves on the plantation and hid them in the cane brake, to keep them from being carried off by the Indians as they returned to the

Nation. This was corroborated by several of our old family negroes who are still living and who testify that it was about 4 oclock P.M. on the day the fort was taken, that Weather-ford came to the plantation and carried them all off, and hid them in the cane. David Tate and full sister of Weather-fords was in fort Pierce when Fort Mimes was taken. Fort Pierce was about ½ miles from Fort Mimes. My mother in law (Mrs Tate) lost two sisters in Fort Pierce when the Fort was taken, and I have often heard her say that Weatherford had told her, that as soon as he was satisfied that the Fort would fall, that he rode off, as he had not the

[p. 62[7]]

7

heart to witness what he knew would follow, to wit, the indiscriminate slaughter of the inmates of the Fort. There are many incidents related of Weatherford, which go to show the nobleness of his nature Amongst them was the daring act of arresting (single handed) the murder and desperado Tallier, who had wantonly and without cause, murdered in cold blood, an old man who was unable to defend himself. Tallier defied the civil authorities, and swore that he could not be taken. The magistrate was powerless as Tallier had defied his posse comitatus, and swore he would kill the first man who approached him and not one would go to his arrest. Weatherford was present, and offered to take him single handed. He approached Tallier who cowered beneath his eagle eye, and submited to Weatherford who tied him, and carried him to Claiborne and delivered him to the authorities at that place. He was always to be found on the side of the weak and defenseless, and from the first days of his manhood believed that his people's rights had been trampled upon by the whites, but nevertheless he was

[p. 62[8]]

8

opposed to his people Joining the British in a war against the U. S. He used all the powers of his eloquence to induce them to remain neutral; told them that when the Americans were weak, and unprepared for war, they made the British Lion howl, and drove him back to his den, that now the Americans were strong, and would be more certain to conquer again, That it would be ... to his people to Join either side, That both the Americans and English were their enemies, that England talked to them with a forked tongue, as did the Americans, That the Palefaces were the enemies of the Red Man, and cared not for his welfare, or distruction, That he was willing to lay down his life for his people if it would benefit them; and drive the white man from their country, but that he was satisfied this would not be accomplished by their Joining either side. These were some of the arguments he used to induce them to remain neutral. This speach was made in presence of Tecumshe, at the time he visited the Southern Indians to get them to Join the Indian Confederacy, to exterminate the Whites. Jimboy,

[p. 62[9]]

9

Big Warrior, Little Prince, and several other of the leading chiefs, favored the views of Tecumshe. But Jimboy and Big Warrior, backed out; Weatherford said they failed to Join the Hostile ... I will now give you some of the reasons which obtained with Willie Weatherford, to cause him to Join the Hostiles against the Americans. Himself and Sam Moniac his brother in law who had married Weatherfords sister Elizabeth) had gone to Chu... of originally. When they returned they found the Warriors in council, where they had decided to Join the British. They had been influenced to take this course by Tecumshe and his prophet, Seekaboo, who was a Narpicanalla chief who spoke good English. (I spell Tecumpsee as the Indians pronounced it,) Tecumshe. The Indians had Weatherfords Wife & children and threatened to put them to death if he did not Join them. He made them the speach as above stated, and when he found that they were determined to go to war he told them that they were his people, that he had been born and raised amongst them, that he would cast his lot with them, though he believed it would be the

[p. 62[10]]

cause of his ruin, as well as that of his people. He told General Woodward after the war had closed, that the great reason why he Joined the Hostiles after he found that his wife & children had to go to war, was, that he believed that in many instances he could be the means of preventing the Hostiles from committing depredations upon defenceless citizens: particularly, women & children. And from this he believed that the Americans would not thank him for ... them, and would no doubt attribute it to cowardice, as they did with many Indians who had done so. In surrendering to Genl. Jackson he did it from a magnanimous and lofty patriotism, he did it to save his people from certain and impending ruin. At what period of the worlds history was there a great and grand patriot and Hero, who performed a greater act of Heroism. He had every reason, to believe that, in surrendering to Gen. Jackson, that he was signing his death warrant, for in the event that Jackson did not have him put to death for his participation in the terrible massacre of Fort Mims, that

[p. 62[11]]

11

the survivors and friends of those who perished there, were thirsting for his blood, and would seek the first opportunity to reek their vengeance upon him. Death stared him in the face on all sides, yet he went forward and offered himself as a sacrifice to save his people. I have often heard the account of his surrender to Jackson, from one who was partly raised with him. It was a follows. After Weatherford had determined to give himself as an offering, or hostage, for his people, He rode boldly forward to Jacksons camp. He was dressed in full Indian costume, and as he approached the camp, he met several officers outside of the lines, they did not know him, and supposed him to be one of the friendly Indians who were often passing in in and out of the encampment. He inquired of a sentinel for Jacksons Headquarters; as he rode up to Jacksons tent. Col Hawkins the Indian Agent was sitting before the tent, and instantly recognized him, and exclaimed, "By the great Alexander, here is Weatherford". Jackson sitting in his tent waiting and immediately sprang from his seat and came out, sword in hand. The news

[p. 62[12]]

12

news spread throughout the encampment like wildfire and the officers from all parts of the encampment rapidly approached Jacksons tent whilst from the soldiers came the cry of, "Kill him, hang him, shoot him." Col. Hawkins introduced him to Jackson and Jackson introduced him to the other officers as they came up. Jackson appeared to be somewhat excited at the ... and further exclamations of the soldiers and swore by the "Eternal" that not a hair of his head should be harmed whilst under his protection, that he was a brave man, and should be treated as such. Weatherford told him (Jackson,) that he (Jackson) was a great warrior and that he had fought him as long as he could, but that many of his warriors were slain, that their bones lay upon many battlefields, that it was useless to contend against him, and ... that could he animate the bones of his dead warriors he would, ... still, said, he knew that he was condemned by many, but he was not ashamed of what he had done, and did not fear death. That he had come to offer himself as a hostage for the future conduct

[p. 62[13]]

13

of his people, That Jackson could do with him as he saw proper, that he had done Jackson all the harm he could. After he had concluded, Jackson took him warmly by the hand and took him into his tent, where they spent the night together, in talking over the incidents of Weatherfords eventful life. Weatherford said that Jackson had a Jug of rum in his tent, and that Jackson put it on the table between them, and that they shook hands and handled the Jug many times during the night. All who were present when Weatherford made his speach, or talk, were struck with the dignity and grace of his action. He was entirely uneducated but was a natural orator, and tis said by those who have heard him in the council, that his burning eloquence enchained all hearers. He spoke the English language with great propriety, and astonished those who conversed with him, when they learned that he had no claims to an education. I will here relate an incident of Weatherford, as told by Judge _____ a distinguised citizen of Mobile. He said that when he was a young man, and reading law in Mobile, his

[p. 62[14]]

14

health failed him, and the doctors advised him to get a horse and take a trip into the country. He said crossed the Alabama river at Montgomery Hill in Baldwin Co. and started to go to Claiborne in Monroe Co. He went by Montpelier where David Tate (Weatherfords half brother) was then living, he had a letter of introduction to Tate, was very kindly received, and hospitably entertained by Tate. In the course of conversation he asked Tate if he knew any thing about the history of "that bloodthirsty monster Weatherford," and where he then was &c. Mr Tate replied, that Weatherford was his half brother, that he was then at his house on a visit, had been there for some time, and had just come in, and was then in an adjoining room, and that he would take great pleasure in introducing him to Weatherford. The Judge said that he began to feel pretty wild, had some serious misgivings about loseing his scalp &c. Dinner was announced in a short time, after they were seated at table, in walked Weatherford with the step and courtly grace of Prince (as the Judge had it). The Judge was introduced to Weatherford by Tate. Weatherford seated himself

[p. 62[15]]

15

opposite the Judge. Whilst they were eating, the Judge conceeded to take a good look at Weatherford, and raised his eyes for that purpose, and as he did so, he found the "eagle eye of Weatherford resting upon him with an intentness of gaze that made him drop his eyes upon his plate, and he again thought of the dubious security of his scalp. The gaze was a bit of mischief and humor gotten up by Tate, as he had discovered that the Judge was not much acquainted with the history of Weatherford, and not informed as to the relationship which existed between them. This incident took place a few years after the war had closed, and the Judge was not living in Mobile during the war. The Judge had designed to spend a few days with Mr Tate but the close proximity of the bloodthirsty Weatherford caused him to change his mind, and after dinner he informed Mr Tate that he had very important business in Claiborne, which required his immediate attention. When the Judges horse was brought out, Mr Tate informed him that his brother (Weatherford) would go with him and assist him to cross Little River, which was between there and

[p. 62[16]]

Claiborne. Holy St Patrick, there was a fix, however with many misgivings as to the crown of his head, he could not then back out, they started, and when the arrived at little at Little river Weatherford told the Judge to take off his saddle and cross on a foot log, and catch the horses as the came out on the other side. The Judge said that he had never unsaddled or saddle a horse in his life, but that he would lay a wager that he unsaddled his horse as quickly as any hostler in Mobile could do it, said that if dispatch in promptly obeying the bloodthirsty monsters commands did anything in the way of security for his scalp, he had accomplished that end. After they had crossed Little River and had gone a short distance, Weatherford bid him good day, and left him. The Judge said, that he never bid a man as harty good day in his life, said he afterwards became well acquainted with Weatherford, and was charmed with his kind and cordial deportment. The Judge said that he never had seen but two men that he could not look square in the eye, and them two men were, Daniel Webster, & Bill Weatherford.

[p. 62[17]]

After close of the war, Jackson invited Weatherford to go to the Hermitage with him. Weatherford went with him, and remained there nearly two years, until after the excitement incident to the war, and the massacre of Fort Mims, had partially died away in the neighborhood of this terrible event. Jackson presented Weatherford with two fine horses, which Weatherford brought home with him, one of which he presented to Captain Hardin, of the U. S. Army. In regard to Weatherfords celebrated leap from a bluff on the Alabama River, I will give it to you as I got it from Mr William Hollinger of this county, ... who had it from Weatherford himself. Weatherford was surrounded on all sides by a company of cavalry, and his only chance of escape was to take the river. He was riding a fleet and very powerful black horse that was perfectly under his control, and (as Weatherford expressed it) "could make him go anywheres." He selected a place where the water from the hills had cut a gully down to the river bank he rode down this gully until he came to the edge of the bank, which was here about 12 feet high. by this time the dragoons had surrounded him on all sides,

[p. 62[18]]

above and below, and several shots were fired down the gully. He grasped his rifle in his right hand, and spoke to his horse and gave him the spur after facing him towards the bluff. the horse sprang forward and made two desperate bounds or leaps. the second one carried him full ten feet clear of the bank, into the river, the horse going entirely under the water, and carried Weatherford down with him up to his waist. The gallant horse arose in a few seconds and struck out for the opposite bank with Weatherford upon his back. after he had gotten about thirty yards from the bank from which he had leaped, the troops on on the bank above and below him commenced firing upon him, and he heard one of the troopers shout, "dont shoot him, dont shoot him," but they continued to shoot at him until after he reached the opposite bank, the balls striking the water on both sides of him whilst he was in the water, one ball cutting out a bunch of his horses mane. He said that he felt more anxiety for his horse than he did for himself as he was much attached to the noble brute who had shared with

[p. 62[19]]

19

with him many hardships, and carried him safely through many perils. As soon as he reached the shore on the opposite side of the river he dismounted and took off his saddle and examined his horse to see if he had been struck by any of the balls; he then wrung the water from his saddle blanket and replaced his saddle. He then made a gesture of defiance to the troopers, and shouted to them to come over, mounted his horse and disappeared. Had I time and space I could relate many startling incidents of this extraordinary, and I might say, wonderful man. Take him all in all, he was one of the most remarkable men of his race, or time, and in connection with this declaration I will state, that in 1837 I heard Dr Webb of Greensboro Ala. say, that he had heard General Jackson say, that he looked upon Weatherford as one of the most remarkable men he had ever met, and that he was emphatically the "Marshal Ney" of the Red Man on this continent, and the elements of greatness so prem-eminent in his organization and character, that had he lived under different circumstances he would have made an indelible mark upon the page

[p. 62[20]]

of history. For courtly and knightly sentiment and demeanor, he was the peer of any man with whom he had ever had intercourse with. That he had personal intercourse with him under his own roof at the Hermitage for nearly two years and the more he saw of him the more he was impressed with the conviction that "Nature had certainly singled him out as one of her special favorites in concentrating in him ... of the ... great man which wer ... our admiration." Weatherford was possessed of a large property in land, slaves, horses and cattle. He owned two plantations on the Alabama river, and after the close of the war, spent most of his time in attending to his farming interst, and stock. He has two sons still living in this county, named Charles and Alexander. Charles is his oldest child, and is now 72 years old. In nobleness of character and all which goes to make up the true man, he has not a superior. He has always been highly respected and esteemed by all who know him. Receiv'd the rudiments of an eductation in boyhood, is a man of fine sense and business capacity. Had

[p. 62[21]]

a fine property in land and slaves when the war commenced, but like thousands of others in like circumstances, was ruined by the war, and is now poor, and has to labor for his daily bread. Alexander is about 56 years old, and in personal appearance, said to resemble his father. He is a man of fair education, and always ocupied a respectable position in society. He had another son named William, who went to the Creek Nation beyond the Mi, about 25 years ago, and has not been herd of for many years. He is supposed to be dead. Weatherfords youngest sister Rosannah, is still living. She is now 70 years old, lives at Mt Pleasant, in Monroe county in this state, she is truly a remarkable woman. Was educated in North Carolina, was said to be one of the most beautiful women of her day, and noted as well for her lovely character as for her personal beauty. She married Capt. Joseph Shomo of the U. S. Army, by whom she had seven children, four of whom are still living, in Monroe Co. They, like their mother, have ever been highly esteemed for their strict integrity and high moral character. Her eldest son is a physician of high standing in his profession, is a gentleman

[p. 62[22]]

22

of culture and high standing, esteemed and respected by all who know him, for his strict integrity and manly traits of character, and I may truly say, that no gentleman in Monroe county ocupies a more enviable position in society. Her youngest son is a farmer, a man of education and fine sense, and like his brother, respected by all who know him. Her other two children are daughters, and like their brothers, esteemed by all, for their moral worth, their lovely dispositions and purity of character and personal charms. Their mother reminds me of some of those grand old ladies of the olden times. All are impressed with the gentle and quiet dignity of her manners, and feel that they are in the presence of no ordinary woman, and no one in our community where ... has lived, has commanded a higher respect from all who knew her. Weatherfords brother John, did not Join him in the war. He was fair and would have passed for a pure white man, was tall and commanding in appearance, Always dressed with a great deal of care, and paid a good deal of attention to the adornment of his person, and had more the appearance of a gentleman of elegant leasure, than a "man of blood". Was

[p. 62[23]]

23

a man of some education, and general information, of strict integrity, of fine presence, gentlemanly deportment and high respectability. Was genial and cordial in disposition, and a gentleman in every sense of the word. He left a family of three children, two of whom are still living, a son and daughter. They are educated and intelligent, and have always ocupied highly respectable social positions. Next to Genl Alexr. McGilvery, the most prominent man amongst the Indians and early settlers of this country, was my wife father, David Tate. He was a man of great natural abilities, was well educated and a man of general information, of large means, and being the nephew of McGilvery, exerted a greater influence over the Indians than any other man in this country, after McGilvery died. His views and opinions in regard to the policy of the U. S. Goverment in regard to the Indians, was indorsed and respected by the Goverment, and went far to shape its course in negociations with them. His influence over the Indians was greater perhaps than that of any other man. He was very reserved, and rather austere in his manners to strangers, but very cordial with those with whom he was acquainted provided

[p. 62[24]]

24

he had confidence in their sincerity of purpose, and I presume I can say with safety, that there was no one who did more for the early settlers of this part of Alabama than David Tate, and his memory is still held in high estimation by all who knew him, and particularly those who had recd aid at his hands. A special act of Congress was passed for his benefit (in 1820 I think it was) and the General Assembly of Alabama passed a similar act for his relations and descendants in 1855. He died at Montpelier in this county in 1829. He left four daughters, the youngest of whom is my wife, And if it was not oversteping the bounds of modesty, or good taste, there is nothing that I could say in commendation of any lady in the land that I could not with truth say of my wife, and her sisters. And in connection, I hope I may be pardoned for quoting the language of one of the most distinguished ladies of the South, who in in speaking of my wife, said, that in her veins runs the very best blood of the South. Weatherford died in 1824, and was burried (within three miles of where I am now living) on the spot where he campted

[p. 62[25]]

25

with his warriors on the night before he attacked Fort Mims. His Mother (Sehoy) his brother John, and several other relations sleep by his side.

The following Memorial was prepared for his tombstone, by Judge A. B. Meek of Alabama.

A Memorial,
of
William Weatherford,
Head Chief Warrior, and Orator,
of
The Creek or Muscogee Indians,
in
The War of 1813 and 1814
under
General Jackson

A True Patriot he defended his
Beloved Alabama,
With the greatest Courage Genius and Eloquence,
And never yielded whilst a hope remained."

The battles of Fort Mims, the Holy Ground, Tohopeka, and the Horse Shoe, with many others distinguished in history, witnessed his prowess, and his misfortunes. His defeat was the downfall of his Nation. His famous speach to General Jackson, is the finest specimen of aboriginal eloquence and saved the sad remnants of his tribe.

After the war he resided near

[p. 62[26]]

near this spot were he lies buried, until his death, honored by all who knew him.

He was born at Talisee in Ala 1774. Died at Montpelier in this State 1824 Leaving many children and relations, who intermarried with the present population.

Though fierce his deeds and red his hand,
He battled for his Native land.
Forget his faults, his virtues know
A Patriot warrior sleeps below.

General Alexander McGilvery was connected with an extensive trading house, of the firm of "Panton Forbes & co." located in Pensacola, and after his death there was some litigation growing out of his interest in the firm, and in this way the standing and title of his father (Lauchlin McGilvery) was ascertained. He was a Scotch Nobleman, of the House of Drummanglass. The Hon John A. Campbell of New Orleans, I think was the attorney in the case, and furnished this information. Weatherfords sister Eliza-beth married Sam Moniac, a half breed, a descendant of a Holender, who came into the Creek Nation in the middle of the seventeenth

[p. 62[27]]

27

century. Sam Moniacs mother was the youngest sister of Oceola the celebrated Florida chief. David Tate Moniac, a son of Sam Moniacs, and Nephew of Weatherfords, was a graduate of West Point. He distinguished himself in the Florida war of 1836. He was promoted for gallantry to the rank of Major by brevet, and was shortly after killed in a battle with the Siminoles, commanded by Oceola, his uncle. David Tate Moniac, left two children and his wife who are still living, and all highly respectable citizens of this county. Sam Moniac visited General Washington in company with Gen McGilvery, and Washington presented him with a medal, which Moniac wore until he died in 1836, when the medal was burried with him. Moniac was always a true and consistent friend of the whites, though he married Weatherfords sister, and Weatherford & himself, were great friends, before and after the war. I will here relate a daring deed of Weatherford and Moniac. There was a man by the name of Bowles who came into the Nation, and represented himself to the Indians, as a British Col. He raised a large body of Indians to go to war against the Spaniards. The Spanish authorities at St Marks,

[p. 62[28]]

Bowles Taken by Weatherford, &c.

28

St Augustine, Pensacola and Mobile, complained to our Goverment, and expected the Goverment of the USA to prohibit Indians residing within her limits, to make encroachments upon their teritory. Col Hawkins (the Indian agent of the USA, was instructed to arrest Bowles. The Agency was then at Pole Cat Springs, in Macon County. Hawkins took Bob Walton (known as the swamp singer) Old Mad Dog, Weatherford and Sam. Moniac. Weatherford was then quite young. As they approached the camp of Bowles, the Indians (under Bowles) presented a menacing attitude. Hawkins told them that he wanted to hold a talk, and after his talk, they could shoot him if they wished. Hawkins told the Indians that Bowles was a bad man, and would bring harm upon them, that he had come to take him, and that they must give him up. The Indians began to murmer and presented their guns, when Weatherford and Sam. Moniac, steped boldly forward and seized Bowles and tied him. Hundreds of guns were cocked but the daring of Weatherford and Moniac, startled and cowed the Indians, and Bowles was carried off a prisoner, and Weatherford & Moniac

[p. 62[29]]

29

carried him to Mobile in a canoe, and delivered him over to the spanish authorities, with a letter from Col Hawkins. An old negro named Jonah, belonging to my wifes father, carried a letter from Col. Hawkins to the Governor of Florida, at Pensacola, notifying the Governor of the capture of Bowles. Gen Thos. Woodward informed me that Col Hawkins told him, that for inflexibility of purpose, reckless daring, and consumate skill in executing whatever he undertook, that Weatherford was without a peer, That no one but Weatherford with the limited means at his command, could have contended as he did, with the force brought against him, to subdue him. And then he was overpowered, and not conquered, or subdued. That he only surrendered for the good of his people, that he believed that if he had thought could have accomplished anything by it, he would have fought Jacksons whole army single handed. The Grand old Sachem of all the Creeks, or Muscgee Indians, was James McQueen. And there is scarcely an Creek Indian of the present day, who has not some of McQeens blood in his veins. McQueen was a Scotchman, and came into the Creek

[p. 62[30]]

Nation in 1716. He said he was in the British Navy, in the service of Queen Ann, That the vessel landed at St. Augustine, that whilst on shore he struck one of the Officers of the vessel, and fled to the Creek Nation, and took an Indian woman for a wife, and from him sprang all the McQueens and their descendants, now in the Creek, and Cherokee Nations. And the McQueens and their descendants are now as leaves in the forest. Oceola was a grandson of James McQueen. Opotholahola, the present speaker of the Creeks, is a descendant of McQueens. The McIntoshes, Rosses, Ridges, and in fact nearly all the prominent Indians now in the Cherokee and Creek Nations, are in some way connected with the McQueen stock. I must now draw this hastily written and imperfect sketch to a close, as the bread and meat question is the one which commands all of our leasure time in this poor, unreconstructed Pachalie, at this time. I could tell you of one John Hague (White) who was captured by the Indians on the frontier of Pensylvania when a child before Bradocks defeat. How Hague raised a son by a white woman at Detroit, who took his mothers name of Girty, and was called

[p. 62[31]]

31

Simon Girty. How this same man Simon Girty contributed to General St Clair's defeat in 1791. How this same John Hague raised a family of children by an Indian woman, and how the youngest son was the bloodthirsty and renouned "Savannah Jack", who no doubt was the most relentless foe the white man had in the Creek Nation. Even after the war closed, it is said he never let an opportunity pass, to kill or whip a white man. I have two old family negroes, who knew Savannah Jack, well, and they coroborate the statements about the implacable hate that Jack entertained for the white man. And they say that the only man that Savannah Jack was afraid of, was, "Mass Billy Wederford" (Weatherford), and him not much. I may resume at some other time.

I have the honor to be,

Very Respectfully Your obt. Svnt.

I. D. Dreisbach

P. S. Gen McGilverys youngest sister, Jennie, Married a French officer, and was taken to France, and all traces of her have been lost.

[p. 63]

George Stiggins & Manuscript Account of Creek Indians.

... Oct. 1st 1873

... of the 13... died. ... I tried ... neglect.

... that my business ... it was not in my power to obt... write to send the manuscript ... Send it with a brief ... appear ... consequent (on ...), at one time accompanying ...

[p. 63[1]]
relating to his career, from Some disinterested persons with whom he was intimately acquainted, and as there are no such persons residing in this community I Shall have to write, in order to do ... I intend calling of a gentleman in Mobile who was very well acquainted with him. Of course there are some here who are acquainted with him traditionally as a character, but none formally.

Should this retard the progress of of the volume you wish to publish I Shall regret it very much indeed. Rest assured I will attend to this as soon as practicable.

Concerning a manuscript copy of Gen. Woodward in a letter Stated, that he had loaned my father, I assure you and that with regret, that I am wholly unable to send you any information concerning it. The migt have had such an article in his possession, if he did it is probable that he loaned it to Some friend, and thus have lost it.

Accept my sincere thanks for the interesting reading matter you sent me. Rest assured they will meet with a just appreciation, but my

[p. 63[2]]
Mother being quite feeble with age does not place a high estimate on books; but, if you feel inclined to present them to me (as I have a large family and all fond of reading) I will give her Something for them as an equivalent, and Something She will appreciate. If all this work provse of any value to you and there is any benefit to be derived therefrom, I wish her to enjoy it as she has preserved the Manuscript.

I decline writing to your friend of Mobile. I respect you as a gentleman of honor, and can trust to your integrity and good intentions.

With many kind wishes for your wellfare and the

prosperity of the Society, I subscribe myself,

Your Sincere friend,

J. N. Stiggins.

[p. 64]

Mt. Pleasant, Ala. Jan 3rd 1874.

Hon L. C. Draper Corr. Secy,

Dear Sir,

I received you favor of the 10th ult a few days since. It proceeded the books 3 days. Nos 3, 4, 5, 6, & 7 reached us in good order; but I am sorry to inform you that that the other 2 have not as yet arrived. I hope they are not entirely lost. Accept my sincere thanks for the nice and valuable presents.

I trust it will not be long before I Shall be able to Send you the old MS; als, the other article relative to my father.

Do not become discouraged. I Shall certainly Send them.

For information concerning my father, I refer you to Dr. Mabin of Claiborne, Monroe Cou, Ala. Also, Col William Boyles of Mobile. As Dr. Mabin is quite aged, he may deem it rather an intrusion on his time & attention, and not respond promptly.

[p. 64[1]]

Col. Boyles, I think, will prove a ready informant.

Yours truly

J. N. Stiggins.

[p. 65]

Mt Pleasant Ala. Feb 5th 1874

Mr. L C Draper Corr Secy.

Honored Sir

I wrote you on the 3rd ult & as you have not replied, think perhaps my letter has been miscarried. & as such may be the case, I will restate. As regards information concerning my father. I refered you to Dr. R Mabin of Claiborne Ala. also, Col William Boyles of Mobile. I also informed you that 2 of the parcels you sent me last, did not, nor has not as yet arrived.

I mail the Manuscript, & other papers to day. Hope they will reach you in good order.

I have been reading General Woodward's Reminiscences of the Creek Indians. In his letters he alludes to the same papers you wrote to me about. He says, he loaned my father his manuscript and other papers. Now, Woodward accuses Col. Pickitt of inaccuracy. I know that he Woodward is not correct in every statement. Tis highly improbable that my father would have borrowed such a document & destroy it, or, loan it to some one else. I knew him too well. He did neither one. He was very careful with papers of any kind; especially valuable ons.

I was a man when he wrote his MS. & had he have had such a thing in his possession, would have been apt to have taken notice of it.

Mother has no recollection of such an article.

[p. 65a]
A short time previous to my removal to this place & about a year subsequent to his decease; I looked over all his papers; & am certain that the ones alluded to by Gen. Woodward was not among them.

I think father derived the greater part of his knowledge of the Creeks from his parents. His father was an intelligent man, & lived & traded among them at least 20 years. My father kept a diary for Historical purposes, from the time, or, before he attained to manhood.

I see in another letter, Gen Woodward sais that Col. Pickett, (giving his author, Mr. Driesbach) borrowed this Manuscript, when he wrote his history of Ala. Another mistake. Col Pickett called at my house (as he sais he did) & look over it about an hour. He wished to borrow it, but said if I were not willing, he would not copy from it. I dont believe he did. Pickett was a high toned gentleman; & his word could be relied upon.

I presume he wanted it to compare with his own History, & to see if they agreed.

Your Sincere friend,

Jos. N. Stiggins.

P S One more little matter & I shall have done. I send you a poem composed by my daughter, to the Memory of her Grand father. She is 19 years old.

If you will be so kind as to correct, & publish it at the close of the Sketch, you will confer a lasting favor, on your

Southern Friends.

[p. 65[1]]

1

My grandfather, Joseph Stiggins, was born in the State of Virginia, on Rhonoke river. Came to this place then the Mississippi territory in the time of the Revolutionary war.

How, or, where the idie originated that he was a Scotchman; I can form no conjecture.

He was a Virginian by birth, of English descent. Was an Indian trader. The trade being carried on chiefly between the Indians & Spaniards.

While engaged in this business, he married an Indian woman of the Natchez tribe, a Mrs. Nancy Grey, a widow. Her Indian name I never learned. She had 2 sisters.

One of whom married a man named Quarlles; the other a man named Proctor. Both white men.

Those 3 sisters were neices of the King of the Natchez tribe; the government being Monarchial. My father by right of primogeniture (being the the next male next heir) would have succeeded to the throne, had he have accepted; but he would have declined all such honors, if honors they could be termed.

My father George, was the oldest child of the 5. He was born in 1788 in this state, where the town of Talladega now stands.

He had 3 sisters: Mary, Susan, & Nancy, and one brother named Robbert, the youngest child. Very little is known of their early childhood.

[p. 65[2]]
2

About the year 1800 my grandfather located near Tensaw river nearly opposite Mobile, & within a mile of the demarcation line between the Americans & Spaniards.

He was the first justice of the peace at that place in which capacity he served several years.

Father was placed in school at an early age, and kept there the greater part of his time till quite a man.

His father did not believe in the popular mode of educating children from home, or, at boarding schools; besides, not having sufficient means to enable him to send all his children from home, & there being at that time no good schools in the then unsettled, or, uncivilized territory, consequently, he sent to Mobile, or elsewhere & procured competent teachers & had his children instructed at home.

I presume his education was as good as the times and circumstances would allow.

Do not pretend to be a judge myself in this matter;

but have heard others say, who ought to be, that he had a good practical English education. Had some knowledge of the Latin language. Could speak the Spanish dialect. The former he studied as a science, the latter he acquired by practice having frequent intercourse with the Spaniards. Understood Creek & Natchez, the latter being his mother tongue, though he could speak neither one fluently.

[p. 65[3]]

3

My grandfather was an educated man for the times. Spoke good English. Could converse in Spanish, Creek, Cherokee, & Natchez.

He was a kind hearted man; have often heard my father tell how devotedly attached his children were to him. They venerated him. He was a fond and doating parrent & provided for his family every comfort, & educational advantage his moderate income would afford. Father was well acquainted with the manners & customs of the Indians; but like all other people of mixt blood, was reared rather white man like.

He was 5½ feet high; Stout; & very corpulent, with a Slight stoop of the shoulders. His average weight was about 220. Head finely shaped; with full hazel eyes. Small hands & feet. Was a farmer, though I cannot say a very successful one.

I am of all the most unsuitable for this task; however, I shall state what I believe to be facts.

In his intercourse wiht his fellowbeings he was kind & affable, possessed a warm & genial nature & one capable of the highist social enjoyment. Was a great talker, & never at a loss for a subject; and as his conversational powers were of A high order, his house was often frequented by the curious & learned.

New & told many interesting anecdotes.

[p. 65[4]]
4

He was neither ambitious, nor avaricious, regarded the former trait when it led to a desire of glory as the latter, beneath the dignity of man. Could not be corrupted with bribes.

He lived in stiring times; could have had great influence among the Indians, had he wished it. He was honest to a fault, but rather impetuous in his youth, but this trait gave way in his riper years.

When quite a youth he joined the Buccaneers who had formed a secret plot for the purpose of taking Mobile from the Spaniards.

His father extricated him from this dangerous affair, as he was not of age. He did not engage in this perilous business, expecting any pecuniary profit; but from a mere love of adventure. he was neither covetous of money or honors.

He delighted in beneficence & liberality, but lacked discernment; or was incapable of judging between worthy & unworthy persons. I will relate one instance. Tis unnecessary to give his name, should he even happen to see this, he will remember the circumstance well:

This worthy seemed to be a nice young man, desirous of making his way upward in the world but lacked means to begin with. He found a ready friend in my father, who set him up in business on a small scale. Stood his security. He lost by that man 12 months board 100 dollars in money & 4 negroes.

[p. 65[5]]

He was a little eccentric in his habits. Sleep seemed to come at his bidding. Care or anxiety of mind never robed him of his repose when needed. Could fall asleep instantly when fatigued. Daylight never caught him in bed unless sick. He generally arose 2 hours before day; would read, write & walk all around his plantation before sunrise. He ate but little. Slept but little. Read much. Was blessed with a most retentive memory.

He was a most affectionate husband, kind & tender parent. Always had a pleasant word or joke, for each member of his numerous family. He was a most considerate master, never expecting them to make any more for him than a support. The unfeigned grief of his servants at his death, outspoke eulogies.

He belonged to the order of Freemasonry.

I have stated his virtues & fidelity to the subject forbids that I should omit his errors.

He was a periodical drinker of ardent liquors, though, the propensity to indulge did not come on at regular intervals. He would abstain sometimes for years, but when the time came round or an occasion required, he had no power to resist, & would indulge to an excess, sometimes for several weeks together, then desist, & perhaps not touch it again for months, & even years. Held a drunkard in abhorrence, & often made

[p. 65[6]]

solemn promises of entire reformation. When under the influence of intoxicating drink, he managed his pecuniary affairs badly. Was then a trading man.

I will state one circumstance, the princilal reason

why his family are now in no better circumstances.

He owned a fine tract of land, now, a most valuable plantation, here on the Alabama river. It was given him by the Government, through Gen. Jackson; for, and in consideration of his sirvices rendered during the war of 1812, '13, '14.

Robbert James then a resident of this place, (now dead) gave him in exchange for the said tract of land 6 negros.

At the time the bargain was made father neglected to have it confirmed by an article of agreement in writing. Soon after he moved to Macon County this state.

His sister Mary, widow of Billy Weatherford, died. My father came down to administer on her estate. Thirteen years had then elapsed since he had been intoxicated. Meeting with many of his old friends he must take a social glass. That drinking spree was protracted sometime. He went home, & after his arrival continued to drink. Mr. James was well acquainted with his manner of indulging, & followed him home to have the matter arrainged concerning the land & negros. Father not being at home, I was sent after him. He did not go home; but sent Mr. James word to meet him at such a place. I delivered the message.

[p. 65[7]]

7

Mr. James started immediately. He said to me I remember the words well. Joe; your father by intemperance came very near ruining his family once before; but I intend to fix up this business right, in order to secure you children, I being then 14 or, 15 years old. The article was drawn up, which stipulated that my father was to hold those negros his lifetime; not mentioning his heirs.

Before the clods had well settled on his grave Mr.

James entered a suit against the estate. A long & expensive course of Litigation ensued. We gained the suit in Circuit Court; but he transfered it to the Supreme, where we lost it.

The negros were then 14 in number. Now whether Mr. James intentionally took advantage of the imbescile state of Fathers mind, or, really intended to do the thing that was right, as he said he would; I leave others to judge.

In February 1812 he was happily married to Miss Elizabeth Adcock, of this state.

He served in the war of 1812, 13, 14, belonged to Cpt. Bailys company, under Maj. Beasely. Was not at Fort Mimms at the time of the Massecree. Had gone home on furlough, Mobile.

He took part with the whites, because he thought it right, & his duty.

His father was a white man. His maternal aunts had both married white men; he himself had

[p. 65[8]]
8
married a white woman, consequently, he felt that the whites were his people; but let us not suppose that he was void of sympathy for his unfortunate, but misguided maternal countryman.

At the close of the war he located here at Mt Pleasant, possessed a pretty property consisting of valuable lands, with negros to cultivate it & a fine stock of cattle.

In 1830 he was appointed agent for the Creek nation. Went to the city of Washington 1830, 31, 32. Assisted in forming the Treaty.

About this time, & while negotiating for the Indians, he went on business to the nation. While there, he visited his old aunts.

The king came in his presence, & after the usual

ceremonies, seated himself & crossing his legs, it being customary for the old king to assume this attitude, in the presence of his successor. Father said this made him feel badly; to think that notwithstanding he had taken up arms against them, they were still willing to recognize him as their future leader.

His Sister Mary married Billy Weatherford, the chief; so called in history. His sister Susan Mrs. Hattaway was taken prisoner at Fort Mimms, Hattaway being killed at that place; She afterwards married Absalom Sizemore. His sister Nancy married a man named Coburn, & died soon after, his brother also died when a young man.

This will not be interesting.

[p. 65[9]]

9

In 1831 he moved to Macon County, this State, & settled between Cubihatchee & Line Creeks. the management of his farm, being his chief employment, & being by nature a most retired & unassuming character, enjoyed as much domestic tranquillity as generally falls to the lot of man.

It was here that he wrote his Manuscript, (or, part of a manuscript) though he had been taking notes ever since he was quite a young man.

In his last illness he expressed much regret at not being able to finish it; being the part with which he was most familiar, or, the part which came more immediately under his own personal observation.

In the fall of 1844 his health began to fail though he kept up till the following Spring, his disease being Chest-dropsy, & having the advice of the most eminent physician the country afforded, he ralied sufficiently to resume his task of writing his history. In the fall of the same year, he was again taken down sick, from which he never recovered.

He was a great Bible reader. Expressed a wish to be baptized; but was not. He never doubted the goodness of God; and expressed no fears at the approach of death, heard him say a few days before his departure. It is time for me to die; I am 57 years old & I know that I stall see God.

On the morning of the of November 1845 he calmly departed this life. Was followed to the

[p. 65[10]]
grave by an immense croud. Was buried at the old Cubi-hatchee Baptist Church.

There is nothing there to mark his resting place.

[p. 65[11]]
Dedicated to the memory of my Grand Father;
George Stiggins

Sometimes I think, I,d like to see;
Grand-father as, he used, to be.
And still I know, tis all in vain,
For none to earth; return again.

And, I,m not sorry, for the fall,
I cannot, call, grand-father back.
In mortal flesh, to suffer more
The pangs of death, that now are oer.

Besides I trust the Saviors hand;
Hath led, him, to a better land;
Whare saints are Clad, in robes of white,
And bliss eternal, knows no blight.

For when around, his dying bed;
Dear ones stood, with hearts, that bled,

He, told them, he, feared not, to die;
That God,would bear him, to the sky;

On wings of love, that never fail,
Though friends, and kindred should bewail,
The loss of one, so kind and dear;
That taught all love, and none to fear.

And angels smiled, his soul to greet,
While kneeling, at, the Saviors feet,
That hands of glory, pure and white,
Should place the golden, crown, so bought;

Upon his head; that he might sing,
With angels prais; to God their king.
And showing, spread, his wings so soft;
That by the Saviors," blood was bought:
Fannie S. Stiggins

[p. 65[12]]
Dedicated to the memory of my Grand Father

The sun was stealing, soft within,
One Cold December after noon,
And I sat down, without the din,
To write of one, with in his toomb.

But, Ah! my fancy wanderd wild,
Mid forest green, and gurgling brook.
Whare all in nature, seemed to smile.
And flowers, peeped, gay, from every; nook.

At last I thought the effort vain,
To write such, verses, as I wished",

About Grand-Sire; who long has lain;
Within the cold; grave, damp, and whist.

For I cant think of him as dead,
But vanished, only, from our sight,
Whare flowers, of ease; Compose his bed.
Sprinkled with dewy, dimands bright.

When I think, of him, I, do, conceit.
He Lingers; near, the pearly, gate.
Wishing, his dear ones; as angels to meet.
Crowned with glory, ne,er; to separate.

Fannie S. Stiggins

[p. 66]

A historical narration of the Genealogy traditions and downfall of the Ispocaga or Creek tribe of Indians, written by one of the tribe ~

[p. 66a]

To the Reader

My dear Sir ~

It is entirely through the solicitation of many of my friends who were excited by curiosity, to know somewhat more of the creek Indians than they could hear or see about them, has induced me to compile a historical narrative of which that body is composed ~ I do assure you my Gentle reader that it has been with a degree of hesitation that I have commenced trying a public exposition of a traditional history and genalogy of my woe-worn and pitiable country ~ for the following reasons I could not forthwith under-take such a work ~

firstly being conscious of my inability to produce any thing worthy of the research or attention of the curious and inquisitive mind much less of the disinterested and well informed, which production when read by the latter class, I am well aware would be treated as a dry and threadbare performance, even as unworthy of criticism, but before it recieves such a fatal neglect, I wish it to be taken into consideration that I undertake this work as a man hood-winked, that I have not nor do I see any materials to form or produce a narrative from. I wish it further observed that I have not the choice of a man who takes a pen in hand to write on a well known subject, nor of him who has a chance to read and extract from approved and studied history, guided and assisted by either of the aforesaid cases I would have no hesitation of mind to proceed on the subject ~ but further when I knew the numberless critics that would scrutanize and descant on my defects and pretentions to a historian, illiberally aided by pretenders to more knowledge of the subject that I am entering on, I cannot but pause and think whether I Shall surmount these foreknown obstakles by a candid acknowledgment of my inability as a prelude, for Your particular notice; and steadily persevere in the obscure tract I am about entering in untill I make an exhibition for public disquisition before I relinquish the idea as impracticable ~ I shall have fables and traditions in many cases to surmount, and but few to recount, for the traditions of the Indians have been handed down, through preceding generations ... moral instruction than as information, to elucidate

[p. 66b]
the inquiring mind, I have been in and participated in their debates in council and know the strength information and power of mind that the present chiefs are in possession of, and I never heard any of them traditionally say or suppose that the principal tribe had any origin but here, so they hold

no tradition of emigration from any country that I ever heard but such branches of the national body that I know of who derived their origin elsewhere I shall relate The traditional account of their settlement and Union with the Ispocaga body ~ as it is a matter not common to find an Indian with antiquated curiosities, he will seldom ask a man more than his business and residence, many more questions to an Indian, is in their estimation idle curiosity and impertinence, so it will happen, the more a stranger questions an Indian, the less pains he will take to abide by the truth in his information, and as many travellers through their nation, would suit the denomination of the inquisitive traveller, who among the number of his questions advanced will urge the one least known to the Indian, viz. where the Indians originally resided, what direction or quarter of the world, they came from, these categorical questions being repeated emphatically, will make the Indian in order to rid himself of impertinent importunity enter the marvellous lists, and recount a Fabricated tale as a tradition not heard before, by himself or any one else, invented merely to suit his auditor, which tale said auditor will tell as a national tradition, so there are ever a new set of traditions for the curious and inquisitive traveller ~ in order to steer clear of such a labyrinth of paradoxes I shall take the most probable side of what I have heard them relate, when I can and seek for more ~ I can assert that it is not known by the Indians why the present assemblage of tribes came by the appellation of Muscogie, without the Muscogie aborigines were destroyed or became absorbed in the present tribes and only left their name at their extinction for the present creek or Muscogie body is composed of the following tribes who retain their primitive tongues and customs Viz. the Alabamas, Hitch-eties, Uchies, Puccunnas, Aubihkas, Ispocagas, Natchez, Cowasawdas.

[p. 66c]
these tribes are inseparably united by compact and consolidated by individual and national interest. I shall take the tribes both separately and bodily in detail with their form of Govorment religious customs and manners and the most prominent parts of their history to their downfall with an explanatory Vocabulary of persons names Rivers animals &c.

[p. 66[1]]

1

The first settlement we find in tracing the Alabamas (a branch of the Creek or Ispocoga tribe) is at the confluence of the Alabama river and Tensaw lake near the Town of Stockton in Baldwin County ~ Their settlements extended up the lake & river as far as Fort Mimbs their town sites and other settlements they called Towassee, and at this time they Call that extent of Country Towassee Talahassee which is Towassee old Town ~ The white settlers of the place call it the Tensaw settlement ~ The Indians say Traditionally that at the time of their residence there that they were a very rude barbarous set of people and in a frightful state of ignorance. Their missile weapons for both war and subsistance was a Bow and arrows made of Cane and pointed with flint or Bone sharpened to a point, with the same weapons they repelled their foe in time of war, in the winter time they got their subsistance in the Forest, and they made use of them to kill the Fish in the shallow parts of the lakes in the summer Season ~ They say very Jocosely they Consider that at this time were they to meet one of their ancestors armed in antient manner, and dressd. in full habiliment with Buckskin of his own manufactury that it would inspire them with dread to behold his savage appearance. they very often make mention of their Forefathers of that age Calling it the time when their ancestors made an inhuman appearance by which we may judge that the then state of their forefathers has been handed down to them as a very rude and frightful state almost beyond conception ~ They do not pretend to any traditional account, when or for what they emigrated to this distance ~ They have a trdition that many of the inhabitants of antient Towassee for some reason unknown to them were carried off on Ship-Board by the French or some other White people many years since, it must have been in consequence of said interruption when the Towassee settlements was depopulated and Carried off on ship board that the remaining part of the tribe removed up the river and made settlements and Towns Autauga and Towassee in

[p. 66[2]]

2

bend of the river below the city of montgomery where they resided to the Close of their Hostile movements in the year of Eighteen Hundred and Thirteen after the treaty of Fort Jackson and the Cession of their Country they removed up the Tallapoosy where their number at this time would be about two Thousand in three Settlements one above the mouth of line Creek Calld. Autawga one above the mouth of Cubahatche Calld. Towassee and the other on the Cosa river above we,tum,ha Calld. oche,a,bou,faw or Hickory ground._They call their tribe Alabamo But by the other tribes they are mostly calld.che lak cul ga, which is a man that uses an imperfect or mixd. language. the greatest evidence among other occurrences that evinces in my opinion of their antiquated residence in this state is the river bearing their name among all the other tribes of the national body from the junction of the Coosa and Tallapoosy rivers to its junction with the Tensaw lakes at the Town of Stockton ~ and as it is common for the Indians to note or name a thing after any uncommon occurrence I make no hesitation in saying that the Alabamas were found here by the other tribes when they located themselves here, and they named the river Alabama after them in acknowledgement of their antiquity ~ As the present tribe of Alabamas have no tradition of origin or derivation it raises a presumption in my mind, that they had a connection at some distant period with the Chickasaw or Choctaw tribes most probably with the latter, and I may say Consequently that they are a relict of the Choctaw tribe from two other Concurrent sources, firstly the similarity of the tongues they speak which is a mongrel of both and no doubt was ...sated since the connection of the Alabamas with the Creek tribe as they had no grammatical rule to retain it in its original stile or purity ~ Secondly by their living in the country and haveing so extensive a Settlement and Claim without a Competition of the other tribes for a distance

[p. 66[3]]

3

distance of near five hundred miles and no traditional Idea of any other than this where there are so many mounds for the disposal of the bones of the dead, which was the original mode of disposing of their dead among the Choctaws, and still partially practised among them to this day ~ Tho' the alabamas of this time do not practice the mode with their dead they may have quit it since their assimilation with the Creek body as it was singular to the modes of Burial in the other tribes as In all national concerns and public assemblies their head men have the Standing and voice that the Chiefs of the other tribe have while in the assemblies they use the Creek tongue; but in their Local concerns they use their own tongue or Language. They are tenacious of their private self goverment seldom associating with any other Indians, the tongue they speak is similar to and can be understood by the Choctaws Chickasaws Hitcheties and Cowasadas. which five bodies in time may have been one nation, detached by some circumstance and separated finally. The alabamas are generally very honest in their dealings and an inoffensive body of people with but few exceptions, being men of sterling courage ingeneral ... which they manifested by the enterprise and damage they done to the white settlements down the river for they done more murder and other mischief in the time of their hostilities in the year 1812 than all the other tribes together. They have no manner of worship nor no idea of performing or practising any adoration to a supreme being than in Thanksgiving for the new crop of corn which they do annually in a very devout and reverent manner. They believe in a supreme disposer of fate for they are predistinarial, always consoling themselves for any misfortune by saying it was so ordered by the great man above ~ about the year seventeen Hundred and ninety three there was an old Cowassada Chieftain that was called red shoes who was violently opposed to their makeing war on the Chickasaws and as it was determined on contrary to his will he resolved to quit the nation so he and a mulatto man who resided with the alabamas named Billy Ashe headed a party of about twenty families part Cowasadas and the rest alabamas and removed to the red river and tried a settlement about sixty miles up from its mouth, but on trial they were so annoyed and infested by a small red ant that were so very numerous in that Country, that they found it hardily possible to put any thing beyond their reach or destruction, so after living there a few years to

[p. 66[4]]

removed finally from thence to the province of Texas on the river Trinity a few miles from the mouth of said river where they now live ~ The first we know of the Uchies who at this day are a part of the Ispocaga body, were once according to tradition a native of the state of Georgia on a part of the Ogeechee called Uchie Creek which may go by that name yet, that place is about as far as their residence can be traced they no doubt were the most savage of all the tribes which Caused their removal and Settlements on the big and little Uchie Creeks below Gerard in this state. They no doubt being of so savage and wild a disposition was the cause why they continually receded as the settlements of white people approached them, they no doubt can claim a neighborship at some distant day to the Shawanase who resided a bout Savannah at the time the Uchies did on Ogeechee and both tribes may have quit their then abode on the Colonization of Georgia by General Oglethorpe about a Century ago in Savannah where the Shawanose then resided. But as the Uchies could not behold a land of agriculture and Civilization they gradually receded from their fastnesses and haunts, they at length united their destiny with the tribes of Mucogie under whose nurturing hand they bask in the pleasure of freedom. They are more entitled than any other tribe in the nation to the appellation of the son of the forest, being attached to a life of sauntering and loungeing and camping in the uninhabited parts of the wilderness. They are more than the other tribes of the nation in many things if possible, being more indolent, more thievish, more dissipated, and depraved in their morals, they are ever in feud with the other Indians (on account of whose property they reach) for their thefts and other depredations of a prowling nature, from their unsettled diposition, they have very few towns of residence, and of course very few farms. Tho' they are considered as of the Ispocoga body, they are considered and admitted to be a perfectly independant people no cognizance being taken of their actions or manners by the other tribes of the nation. Their dishonesty is proverbial in the nation, so that any remarkable thief is said to be like a Uchie licensed to steal with impunity, in all conversations among themselves or not they speak their own barbarous tongue ingeneral, which is a quick gutteral stammering accent not very unlike the dying respiration of an old sow under the hands of a Butcher. The Uchie tongue is only spoken by the natives of ... tribe, as there is not exceeding four or five instances of its being learnt and spoken by any one else; they are so

[p. 66[5]]

5.

attached to their own Tongue and mode of living that very few of 'em make any use of or can converse in the national tongue, which is said by the other tribes of the nation to be owing to the general dislike expressed and manifested against them, as well as to their wild roguish and insipid nature ~ The Puccunnas at this day are only known by tradition to have been a distinct people and their antient Town or habitation is called Puccun Tal ahassee which is Puccun old town. This antient town is in the present Coosa County of this State. the Au bih kas have a tradition that they were a distinct people and that they in old times were very numerous, but do not say whether they were emigrants or not, or at what time they became one of the national body, but they say as they belonged to the national body one and inseparable, there was no distiction made, so that by continual intermarriage with the other tribes they at length became absorbed and assimilated with their neighbors without distinction and no Lineal knowledge left of them but the name of their antient habitation, whether in Conversation they had a separate Tongue of their own or not tradition is silent. ~

The Au bih ka tribe reside indiscriminately in the Talladega valley with the Natches tribe who they admitted to locate and assimilate with their tribe as one people indivisible a little more than a Century ago; they at this day only pretend to know and distinguish their tribes from the mothers side of descent but they are as one people with the Natches at this time. ~

The Au beh kas of this day no doubt are the lineal descendants of the people who somewhat more than three centuries past so unavailingly and violently opposed the adventurous Ferdinand Soto on his researches through their Country, according to the first historical account we have of them on record, and why may they not by conjecture be entitled to the Claim of the primitive Mucogie more than any other of the tribes, for they are not discriminated by any antient denomination that is known of, for their present appellation is derived from their manner of approveing or acquiesscing a proposition tho' the national tongue is spoken by the tribe in all its purity yet most notorious they assent or approbate what you may say to them inconversation with the long aspiration āw̄ whereas the rest of the nation approbate or answer short c̄āw̄ ~ from their manner of answering, or approbating so singular they got the name of āw̄ b̄ēh̄ k̄ā moreover the rest of the Indians in talking of them and their

[p. 66[6]]

tongue aptly call it the aw beh ka tongue, and never resort to the appelation of Ispacaga only in a national way ~ The au bih ka part of the tribe inhabiting the Valley of Tal adega are lineally descended from the people visited by Ferdinand Soto of Spain in his researches for Gold among these tribes in about the year A. D. Fifteen Hundred and fifteen and from the transcript of preregrination he has left it is evident that they had been residentors for a length of time previous to that date. I will put a quere to the reader with a combination of circumstances for his own conjecture and solution ~ Soto says he was as far north as nickajack in the Cherokees which was so named at that distant time, and of passing through Cosa wa tee which name in the Cherokee language is cosa old town ~ he farther mentions in the Vicinage of his au bih ko che fortification a town called ca sa Tul muchessee which in the Creek or au bih ka tongue is cosa new town, which town stands near the banks of the Cosa river at this time called Kellys Town at what area the Au bih kas resided in Cosa wa tee and why they removed and when they built Cosa tal muchessee tradition is silent whether they did or not ~ but many would say with myself that the au bih kas once resided in Cosa wa tee from whence they were expelld. by the Cherokees, and after their expulsion they made their location in Talladega Valley on the river and named their new in remembrance of their former abode ~ cosa Tal muchessee or cosa new town, I shall make a conjecture that from the aforesaid two towns Cosa river originated its name ~ so gentle reader I have made all my references as a quere and put them before you so you can coincide with me or not ~ the town of au bih ko chees in the Taladega Valley by its name would raise an inference that there was, or had been, a larger town of that name some where, for that name in english is little au bih ka. whether they ever had a larger town of that name, or for why they should so name the town, tradition is silent and I am unable to say. ~ Ferdinand Soto further says that he had a fortified camp near the last named town, which I expect may be relied on as a fact, for in the vicinity of the town on the margin of a large Boiling Spring there is visibly the ruins of a breast work that appears to be of antique date, while he remained in said Breast work he says that he was attacked by the natives of the place Several times, at which time they may have got in possession of a brass drum that was in

[p. 66[7]]
7
their possession not a half century ago kept as a trophy ~ and said by them to have been got by their ancestors in times of old from a people who invaded or past in a hostile manner through their country comeing from up the river that they were not like any people they ever saw before, that they were ferocious proud and impudent in their manners from the traditional circumstance of the brass drum it would lead to the inference that the proud people alluded to, was the escort of Ferdinand Soto, and that the Indians came in possession of one of his drums by some means ~ and most probable he was attacked at that place by the whole nation when and where they may have got possest of six brass trapings or breastplates held in supersticious Veneration by the Tuckabachians of them I will treat hereafter ~ Soto makes mention again of encamping near the junction of the two rivers and names the place mavilla while in which encampment that the Indians attacked him several times in large bodis and when they found themselves unable to make an impression on his camp, they came to terms of peace. I merely infer as I said before that remarable adventures or circumstances would aptly derive a name of note, so the

aforesaid attack and peace, may have transpired at an antient breastwork on the riseing ground nearly opposite the mouth of line creek, near the othle wal lee town called by the white people Cle wal lee as the name of that town is the Division of war, or where they fought and parted, what other notable transaction could have merited a town that name I cannot divine, for I have inquired of men of that town, who I thought had some tradition of that among many others they could relate but got no Clue to alter the above advanced conjecture, so I shall leave it to the next better informed Commentator to solve, and proceed to the natche tribe ~

The Natches the men of that tribe almost all converse in the Creek tongue with their families or not, tho' the women can speak it fluently yet most generally in their own Common Concerns. And to their Children they use their own native tongue, frequently in one house they use both tongues without any detriment to their conversation or business. The tradition they relate as the cause of their removal from the Seat of their nativity, to their final Settlement in the Tal adega Valley I will relate as heard it ~ that about one Century ago that the tribe lived in one large body or tribe Town on the bank of the Mississippi where the present City of natches now stands and extended above it, that their goverment

[p. 66[8]]

8

was monarchial, and that all cases both civil and political was determined By the king and his suit, for he was attended by both men and women in great state. The throne was hereditterry and the king was supreme head of the tribe, his person was sacred and his mandates inviolable, he lived in a retired manner in the suberbs of the town, secluded from society of all persons but his own near relations, who officiated about his person both men and women as attenants and guards, about one third of his connection at a time, and such as were not in attendance on his person, were in the Forest in search of game for his subsistance. during the hunting excursion the party was headed by one of his near relatives to direct and take care of the party. But it must be noticed that all earthly institutions tho' made for lasting happiness for ages, are delusive and visionary so it happened to them, for while they were living under their peaceable and happy institution of govorment a govorment familiarized to them by time, and consonant to their habits of life, they received a visit from a detachment of French who went up the river Mississippi to explore the Country and fix on an eligible spot to erect a garrison and without a previous compact with the natives to ensure their good will, they pitched on a site in the vicinity of the town, tho' much against the will of the Indians they disguised their chagrin and seemingly were careless and not opposed to the encroachment of their unwelcome Visitants and neighbors, who had fortified themselves in the suberb below the town ~ The French by their gallantry, pursued the destructive course said to have been in Sodom of olden time, as the danger was not imbruing nor destruction awfully pending over their ill fated heads. They made free with the men and married their women they were tolerated in their love to their women with seeming good will by the natives for they saw the advantage that would ultimately result through their blind devotion to love, for it would make them unsuspicious and unguarded against a design they had in contemplation to effect through that means, as was expected their lewd practices soon caused a relaxation in their vigilance and discipline, for they frequented the town at night in a careless manner and unguardedly admitted the women into the fortress at night and made them welcome Visitants at all times, the Indians saw how remiss and negligent the French were geting in their manner of living, as was expected, and they for revenge secretly and exultingly proceeded to put their scheme in

[p. 66[9]]
9
execution, which was to exterminate their gallant and unwelcome neighbors ~ Therefore the Indian men concerted a plan with their women as though without design for the women to make their appoinments with the Frenchmen to be and stay within the Fortress on such a night, which appointment was accordingly made and the garrison overreached for when the time arrived instead of the expected women, the fortress was entered by men in disguise and armed who on entrance instantly fell to work and exterminated the whole garrison of men, one man escaped by his loveing wife wishing to save, had prevailed on to stay with her in the tower that night, and after the above catastrophe she effected his escape down the river Mississippi so he carried the news of the disaster of his comrades to his country men ~

The Indians were very much elated with the successful event of their plan which had even exceeded their most sanguine expectations geting clear of their intruders so quickly and easily without the loss of any of their own blood ~ but their joy was of short duration, they equipt themselves with the spoils of their vanquished neighbors, in arms clothing provisions and hats which last they particularly admired and they never had an Idea that there were any more or others to revenge their horrid deed ~ in their enthusiasm to take possession of their empty garrison that they so easily attained they unanimously concluded and even prompted his majesty and all his suit, and all that could get quarters to remove therein as the buildings were more commodious than those of the town ~ Then after they had arranged their new habitation and got all snug and secure, the king sent out the usual hunting party headed by one his nephews but after their hunting excursion was over and they returned, behold their surprise to see a number of shipping moored in front of the Fort and apparently the whole of their tribe in the act of embarking on board of the shipping under the guard and Controul of two rows of white men with hats on similar to them worn by the people that they destroyed, from the following circumstance I expect the whole of the tribe were not captured as there is a people on the south waters of the missouri who call themselves Natchez, who probably made their escape when those in the fortress were surrounded and captured, all that were shipped off by the French were insulated and settled in the Island of Sto. Domingo where their progeny now remain, their arms offensive and defensive were bows and Arrows pointed with either sharpened Bone of pieces of flint ~

[p. 66[10]]

With those weapons they attacked their enemy, or killed their game for subsistance, when those that had been a hunting returned and saw the tribe embark on the shipping and disappear down the river, they could not imagine what would be the result of their distination and fate, so in their incertitude and perplexity of mind they concluded to leave their forlorn case with the seat of their ancestors forever, and in the scene of a new and untried home forget the wreck of their tribe who they expected were doomed to slavery and wretchedness, haveing had an intercourse and friendship with the Chickasaws they made to them first where some took up their abode, and some with the Cherokees, and the great part headed by the royal family made a compact of assimilation with the au bih kas or Creek tribe and settled in the Tallidega Valley they remained thus squandered for about twenty five years when at the instance of their chief they all made their final exit and settled in the Valley and by their compact made a member of the Ispa-caga body to this period. This remnant of the natche tribe to this distant day are unfriendly to the French people ~ Their antient manners and customs it is said was similar to that of the au bih kas so they had to make no change in their habits of life by their removal ~ These statements were handed down to the most antient of the present day by their forefathers who were spectators though in their infancy of what had happened to and in their tribe, they have a belief in a supreme being but no worship or adoration, tho' they generally talk about good and bad actions in this life I never could understand that they had any idea of rewards or punishments in future for they most generally believe in another life here or a place they cannot describe, they keep the Busk festival in a very devout and sacred manner ~ Near one of their towns in the Valley Not very far from Sotos. fortification there is a cavern said to be near a quarter of a mile Long dissected by many divisions such Indians as has been in it say that it is peopled by Fairies they had never seen any because they have the power of being imperceptible but they had seen their tracks and knew that they lived on the innumerable bats and swollows that stay in there. it was entered by some men many years since that is a half century ago they found a humans bones in the first room and right by him carved in a rock, I W Wright 1723 ~ In the address to my narrative I said as a prelude I would intersperse an Occasional Tradition Therefore I will relate one retained

[p. 66[11]]

by the Natches tribe and related by them as a matter handed down through successive generations for their information. I insert it to shew in its connection, an inference that in Olden time their patriarch knew or heard some way of the deluge and that the primary information or knowledge he had of it had got blended with traditional Fiction ~ it is said that speech and rational power was given to man alone and he by his knowledge and understanding is enabled to make the other creatures subservient to him, so that he rules and manages them in a way most conducive to his will and their comfort in life, but when the gift of speech is imparted to a dumb creature it is to be observed as a matter of inspiration to the beast purposed by the great spirit to be words of sacred truth from himself through said creature, as a manifest proof of the foregoing remarks that there was a large assemblage of the antients on some particular occasion in times of yore, when to their surprise they were accosted by a little dog, who haveing gaped and yawned in a particular whining manner, he began in articulate words to bemoan their sudden fate; he called on them individually to look between his ears first toward sunset and then every other direction and see their final termination of life, they looked accordingly as he said but they could see nothing but on a second biding they could see mountains of water rolling toward them he bid them fly to the mountains for safety who could and escape death, so they fled but a few of 'em reached the mountains being overtaken and overwhelmed by the waveing torrent of water. Among them the old man of sorrow was one who escaped by his flight to the mountains ~ he is called in their tongue tum seal hone hone opah he uttered his wailings and lamentations continually and in tears of sorrow he mourned for all that perished, and his sorrow likewise extended to the living who he took under his care and tutored them by good words the best way to live in future to shun the paths of destruction ~ The earth was overwhelmed by the billows of water and no one survived that did not attain the summit of the mountain from these was the earth repeopled ~ Who this old man of lamentation or sorrow was may be a question but as I never heard any more of him, I shall leave him as I heard of him, without any conjecture relative to him, to be solved by the inquisitive, and the antient of days.

While I am in the vein of relating traditions I will insert one of the Ispacoga tribe relating to their former with the Shawanose the part of the nation Calling themselved Ispolaga are composed of the large and Smaller towns on Tallapoosy river to its head and those of the

[p. 66[12]]

chattahochy river excepting the Hitcheties and Uchies ~

It is related that once in times past, that the Ispacaga and Shawanose tribes, made a resolution and formed a compact by which they were thereafter to consolidate their Interests and the two tribes to be but one in future, and perform their yearly custom of thanksgiving and other rights of religious ceremony as one people ~ for they at that lived bordering on each others Territory, the Shawanose in and about Savannah in the State of Georgia so in accord with their compact, they deposited with the keepers of the national square of one of the tribes, their calumet Tobacco Pipes Belts and war club called by them Attussa, with all their emblems of peace and friendship together with twelve pieces of brass described as follows six of them was oval of about (eight inches long and seven in the widest part) and the other six are about (nine inches long and four in width) made square bearing a resemblance to antient soldier breast plates. they all belonged to the Ispocoga tribe, and were (three of the oval and three of the square kind makeing six to a set when exhibited) for they are never exhibited but in their fasting and feasting to commemorate the new Corn Crop, so they deposited two sets of the above plates in their national square according to compact, the United tribes of Ispocaga and Shawanose performed their ceremonies together with concord for a length of time. But through some unknown reason or occurrence which the Ispocagas attributes to the instable and fickle disposition of the Shawanose, who formed a resolution to cecede from the union and national compact and remove, no remonstance of the other tribe against it could alter their determination for they dissolved their union by emigrating northwardly, and when they moved they carried off six of the sacred brass plates three Oval and three of the square kinds, which the Shawanose have retained possession of ever since, for they were seen by some Creeks first in the care of the old prophet at tippacanoe about the time he fought Genl. Harrison and not long since they were still in his possession over the Mississippi, and seen by some Creek chiefs who visited that tribe to whom they were exhibited with a traditional detail of how they came in possession of that tribe with all its circumstances, which account corroborated with the Ispocaga tradition of their loss ~

[p. 66[13]]

13

The Hitcheties live on the Chattahoche river about the mouth of Uchie Creek in a body to themselves but are considered by the other tribes as a part of the national body, in their local concerns and town meetings they use their native tongue, which is similar to the Alabama tongue, being a mongrel of the above and Choctaws tongue they were once seminolas of of Florida, they would number at this time about one thousand their chiefs take rank as the other chiefs of the nation of the same grade. The word Seminola in the national tongue denotes an estray as any beast &c that is strayed from the original stock or fold is called a seminola no doubt the Hitcheties from their speaking a mixed tongue were a seminola from one of the aforenamed tribes ~

I have traced and made an exposition of national genalogy by their tribes as far as information or recollection will serve me at this time. my reason for hitherto haveing confined my narrative only to the Upper creeks as they are called who live on the cosa and Tallapoosy without adverting to the subsisting connection with the other parts of the tribe on the Chattahoche Called the lower Creeks was according to a plan I had in view, which was firstly to treat of them as two independant departments but on reflection I conceived them to be one body with two heads, who consolidates their detached and independant departments for national energy and common Utility. Secondly it would save a tedious and prolix exposition of their local situations and environs ~

Before I proceed on a trial to delineate their form of Govorment I must necessarily mention to the reader that should I in the time of writing this narrative gain any farther light about any of the aforesaid tribes, either of genealogy tradition or custom worthy of notice I shall insert it in an after piece, to avoid digression and confusion in my narrations, as much as possible, not saying that I shall keep clear of prolixity or digression, but my wish is to keep every circumstance conformably circumscribed under its proper head ~

The form of Govorment under which they live is a tyrannical Oligarchy in its principles and practiced under that head to the full extent, at a slight view The most of people suppose and say that it is a democracy on republican principles but it is far different, for all public business whether of a national or private character is done by the chiefs, though the nation is summoned in what is termed their grand council, where the state of the nation is supposed to be examined into

[p. 66[14]]

and their oral laws made. The Assembly say not a word in the matter for while in their sittings the assembled body of the nation sit as mutes without being consulted in any manner untill a few chiefs in their council house make the laws for their goverment without condescending to ask an opinion or approbation in any case, the national body being merely convened to hear what is done, for after a law is digested by the chiefs The national convention is informed of its tendency by the orator of the nation in a very exact and precise manner, who moreover informs them of all that has been transacted, which new law when they are made acquainted with its tendency, let it be as it may, they are the most obedient subjects under the sun to the penalties of it, be it oppressive or not, should they infringe the law they will suffer beating confiscation of their property or Even death without a murmer or family resentment, moreover Should an Indian be obstreperous in contending for his right, of property or otherwise or obtrude on on the right or even interests of a chief, the chiefs can so far tyrannize after a consultation as to have him beat or slain, as a common disturber of the peace without any other imputation of guilt, than a law breaker as they term it ~

in former days in the time of their self importance and undisturbed goverment, before an agent was located in the nation by the U.S. to improve their morals and reform their customs; their ordained chiefs were more rude active and despotic and more frequent in their mandates of tyranny, and not near so uniform and circumspect in their deportment as now toward the common men ~ In latter years the principal Chiefs or great men of the nation have been increased to about fifteen in number their nomination has been approved as such by the agent of the Goverment and recognized as such by all the tribes ~ They are invested with power and authority to superintend the affairs of their national Govorment with the incumbent duties annexed, such as recieving the national salary from the agent of the U. S. and paying their public debts ~ which they seemingly do with a national concurrence ~ for they never undertake or do any important business wiithout a national convention

[p. 66[15]]
when the chiefs deliberate and through their orator inform the assembled body of the nation, of what they have determined and dissmiss them ~

For a better distribution of their public business such as public work of planting and tending in corn &c. their public town field and gathering their Eupon or Cassene leaves for their black drink when every man of age is obliged to attend and do his part or be fined according to his circumstances The inhabited parts of the nation is laid out into town districts designated from some creek ridge or point to some other noted point, which boundary is organized into certain town corporated precincts under the moral guardianship of their <u>mic cul ga</u> which term is the plural of <u>mic co</u> a term of gradation more applicable to the office of overseer or guardian in my conception than to that of a king, (as most of people will interpret it,) as many towns have at least one tenth of its population for <u>mic cul ga</u> which is none too many for guardians to watch over them & moralize their conduct, but it is constituting by far too many kings for one town or principality, when it is thought necessary by the principal men or committee of townsmen to make a new mic co, they proceed very ceremoniously in their rude way to his inauguration, to wit. Without his being previously consulted on the subject, when they have made the determination to effect it, and at their townhouse assembly, they advance up to him, and call him at the same time in a loud long and shrill tone by a name that he is thereafter to go by, with the addition of mic co, for instance such as yo ho lo micco or Ispocoga mic co &c. and at the same time they smear his face all over with white clay ~ a ceremony immitating in importance the accolade of knighthood and Sir ~ Though some of the mic co do rise to be a principal chief it is by his merit, for his nominal office is for town purposes to admonish regulate and keep in peace the members of their town people by whom they are regarded with respect and deference. there are other applicable sir names given to distinguish their grade in their town police, they attend the appointed national calls only as mutes, for in the national assembly none have a voice but such as are appointed to national purposes. their other formalities I shall embrace in the succeeding Chapt.

[p. 66[16]]

Manners and Customs ingeneral

The most prominent and I believe it to be the most uniform feature in their national character which shews itself constantly is in their civility and innocent deportment to each other and especially to a stranger that may travel among them and is sociable and seems to wish to conform to their customs and manners, without being self important or asking too many impertinent questions, which will often disgust them and conclude in bad consequences, to my knowledge they are not a people to utter a remark or word to hurt the feelings of any one, without they should be in a state of intoxication, for should they press a joke even on a friend or acquaintance so far as to be disagreable and likely to ruffle his temper, they will immediately surcease apologise and withhold and it rarely happens to hear one of them at any time reflect on the conduct or reputation of another. if there should be a man of general bad repute it will be taken up and related by one of their mic cos. without pointing out any person in particular, but lay open the ill consequences in any person of such, and such, ill conduct his comments would be more pointed and acrimonious should there be an instance of a person in the town so churlish of his eatables as to be inhospitable to a one of their own people especially to a traveling stranger. such a niggardly person is termed by them a (no body) so of all people they are the most tenacious of their reputation in hospitality for on the entrance of a stranger into one of their huts he is immediately requested to sit down and as an introduction to be his acquaintance he is asked his residence, destination, and business such questions are so common among them that they are replied to satisfactorily and in a brief manner. in the meanwhile he is supplied with eatables, which is uniformly done at every house he may call. their provisions bestowed to an acquaintance or stranger is put forth with a welcome which need not be doubted, should it compose the last morsel that they have got, as the provisions they bestow to a man is one of the links of their chief pride. to doubt his heartty welcome in that case would unutterably hurt his feelings ~

[p. 66[17]]

Though their Custom may be laudable and beneficial as hospitality ever is, but it is with them a tendency both to a good and bad purpose. if it is beneficial in keeping the traveller and stranger from hunger and starvation, it keeps a great many of their town people of men and women sauntering from door to door in loafing Idleness. if no one will clothe them, they are perfectly satisfied for every house will feed them. they are ingeneral disinterested to a degree of negligence either in the distribution of their provisions to eat or the means for the acquisition of it or wealth. They are freee from the inquietude contentions and frauds that so often produce strife and feud, among the interested and careful part of mankind. many years may intervene before you see two sober Indians quarrel about property or any other interesting matter for in their sober moments they seem to be totally disinterested not only to their own concerns, but that all the avenues to lucrative or other passions in them are absorbed in their wish to be social and civil to each other. it is not that their passions are indifferent either to the ease of wealth or possession of property for they are very fond of possessing property if they make no more use of it than the possessing of it, for it is notorious that in consequence of their habitual idleness all laborious pursuits tending to lucrative purposes are thought by them to be beyond their effect, without looking foward for ways and means or even trying, they count the completion of it if attended with the least difficulty unsurmountable and submit it to oblivion. all their difficulties in life is caused by their inaction and want of energetic measures, for I have noticed that they do not lack comprehension in any intricate piece of macanicism haveing an idea of all its points and bearings to effect it, so that their genius for mecanical purposes is of no use to them being paralised for the want of energetic action to put in use their comprehensive ingenuity ~

I think it necessary in this place to contrast two topics of their life and actions at this time that is takeing into consideration their brotherly love and national attachment to each other While in a natural and sober state, and the extremities of the opposite When in a state of intoxication which is now a habit extending from the national Chiefs to the

[p. 66[18]]

poorest dregs of the nation, for when they are in a state of intoxication all personal distinction among them is prostrated with the tenant to the ground, it does make many thinking men view such a scene with horror, and pity on the case when they consider the depravity of the human stability, for chiefs common men and women will wallow in filth and mire so long as they can raise the means to purchase spirits to drink. during such time of frenzy they will fight each other indiscriminately frequently takeing each others lives; and when such fracas is over they attribute the whole scene to the spirits they have drunk, very truly saying it was not them but the liquor that was in them that fought, well knowing and meaning their peaceable disposition toward each other when in their natural state of Sobriety so I leave their pernicious drink ~

as I have gone through the Statement of their pernicious drink I shall now enter on their Uniform custom of Drinking their assee which is a very strong black tea used by them without any sugar, made of Eupon or Cassene leaves. said drink is called by the whitemen among them the Black drink. it is customary at this time and may have been for ages back for the men to meet at their town house or square in every town atleast once a Week & in the Tuckabatchies the principal town they meet every morning to drink their assee, which is prepared for use in the following manner at all places. it is parched first in a large pot of their own manufactory of clay untill the leaves are brown, then water is applied to the full of the pot and boiled by a man appointed to that service. after boiling it is cooled in large cooling pans of the same manufactory by one of the oldest chiefs of the town. when it can be pored over his finger without scalding it is cool anough to drink. it is then put into two gourds that would hold near a gallon each with a hole in it of about three qrs. of an inch in diameter at which hole they suck it out. said gourds of assee is very ceremoniously handed round the square to every man by men selected for the purpose drank as its made without sugar or any other embellishment.

[p. 66[19]]

19

it is a singular thing to think how this tea operates on them after they drink it, for after they have drank it they retain it in their stomack for near a half hour they can discharge their stomack of it again as often as they drink it, with seeming ease, spouting it out of their mouth as it were by eructation after four or five drinks and discharges of their stomack at different times of near a quart at a time. The black drink being over they disperse at or near ten aclock; it acts as a tonic, as it is drank of a morning fasting by the process their stomack is well rinced and braced up. The taste of the black drink is not disagreable to the stomack being not unlike very strong black tea and nearly of a black colour ~ no doubt but their custom of drinking the black drink originated through political motives viz. for the purpose of assembling the towns people frequently at their town house or square in order to keep them united, for the harmony subsisting among the people of a town is noted and seems to be cemented by an affection as strong towards each other as the sons of Jacob of old in their association ~ as the usages and customs of every town is similar and the men all know the unity and simpathy of a town people, the men of one town will approach another town with seeming diffidence though the towns may be contiguously situated, and as such is their practice in this their more enlightened time, their approaches toward each others towns and towards strangers must have been with extreme timidity and Caution in their natural and more savage State ~

and as they seldom change their town site it is probable they are situated as they were at the time of Ferdinand Sotos visit more than three Centuries ago ~

[p. 66[20]]
20
I have observed among them another trait of national Character that is in the public meetings whether for black drink or national council the Indians appear studiously to wish to shew an importance in themselves and independance of character for they will perceptibly assume to themselves a grave sedate consequential deportment, especially their chiefs, and head men. They would appear for a while to a by stander to be careless of all nature and each other. at length nature seems to predominate and shew their true disposition when they commence smokeing their pipe the spell seems to be removd. for after a few draws of smoke from their pipe they cordially hand it the next at hand who has it optional to make use of the contents of the pipe or pass it to the next man which is frequently done by a constant repitition of of such civilities it engenders a familiarity in the community at large by slow degrees that would not have taken place otherwise, as they seldom have any interesting conversation to impart or attend to with a stranger. it is customary with them to use hesitation even

should they wish to converse with him they accost each other with studied and manifest civility to which they reciprocally recieve an answer equally ceremonious and apposite untill an acquaintance takes place.

They in a general way appreciate a good character very little either in themselves or any one else in the common scenes of life as there is no perceptible difference made by them between a discreet virtuous woman and one of ill fame and lewd. practices in the common standing of society. it will equally extend to men for thieves murderers and other evil practitioners are not held in disrepute nor are they subject to either scorn or reproach

[p. 66[21]]

for they very often make head men or miccos of such men so that their actions are in unison with their natural inclinations and only amenable to their customary laws, so far they are the irreproachable and true sons of nature and inclination.

Their Custom of marriage and widowhood

It is customary among them when a man selects the one that he wants for wife frequently without speaking to her or consulting her approbation to open the subject of his wishes for an alliance in their family (or have it done by some of his kins people) to some of her relations though most properly to the uncle of the woman on the mothers side who has entire controul of his nieces in case of marriage or otherwise. should the offer meet his approbation he does not protract his consent or disavowal longer than he can lay the proposal before her relalations of the mothers side who are counted her actual kinsmen and women, in which assembly the candidates disposition and other qualities are discust. the Father nor none of the womans father family are ever consulted in cases of marriage of his children as he nor they are not of the same family; as the primogenitureship of all families descends from the mother. (The above I will explain hereafter). When the uncle or relation has informed the rest of his kindred or Clansmen of the proposal of marriage and by whom made, and that he approbates the proposed match the rest of the family seldom refuse their assent. there is no fuss made of fortune portion or chattels on either side. After such consultation if the suitor Should visit their dwelling before they do him, he is informed of the family acquiessence, and the bridal bed being publicly made for the pair, make a conclusion of the courtship and marriage. after the consumation of the marriage and he finds her in clothes, should she be the first wife formally married to him and passes the Boos ke tah with him she is viewed as his actual wife by his kinsfolks and all other after the solemnization of the new corn feast, passes over them

[p. 66[22]]
22
she is is bound to him in the conception of his family during life or his pleasure that is should She be indolent and given to quarrel with him and inattentive to his wants and disobedient to his commands in any of the aforesaid cases he can make complaint to her family of such and quit her and marry another without a murmer of her clan or family ~ but in case she should prove a lewd woman and inconstant to him, she can be punished by his family or clanspeople by beating her with large sticks untill she cannot move and then cuting off both of her ears close to her head though the punishment may be inflicted contrary to the will or consent of her husband, which frequently happens then after her

punishment for her incontinency it is optional with her husband to repudiate or retain her still as his wife as poligamy is only admitted among the men by the wifes consent. They use a great deal of force and craft to obtain it, in order to keep clear of the crime of adultery. all his after married wives has tostay at their homes without his wife should conclude with herself to let one stay with her in the house & do all the drudgery of the place as a waiting maid by his wifes consent he can take as many wives or concubines a he chooses to maintain, but should his wife disaprove of his having a concubine and he obtain one against her will his wifes relations or clanspeople has it in their power to beat him & his concubine or second wife with sticks and cut off both of their ears, after which he is separated from his wife, and he has to retain the one beaten on his account, nevertheless he has in his power to keep his old wife single for four years or four Boos ke tah without she should elope with a man and elude the vigilance of his clan to the ensuing Boosketah then she is clear of punishment for her adultery even after she is finally separated from him and the controul of his clans women ~ it is customary for the clanspeople not to tolerate the widowed man to play Joke or touch a woman nor a woman a man during their

[p. 66[23]]

as I have gone through their marriages ceremonies and touched on their state of widowhood I think it necessary to inlarge and be more explicit on the subject, therefore after marriage should they live inseparable during their life on the death of either, the survivor is made a widow of in the following manner, viz admitting that the woman should be the survivor immediately after the mans burial, the women on his mothers side connected to him, or his clan women who are all the widows guardians or retainers proceed to divest her of her gay apparel and her other ornaments of dress such as broches beads and neclaces, and unloose her hair and spread it over her shoulders, in which situation she is to remain and consider herself a mourner for four years for her deceased husband, unless she is sooner relieved by the compassion of her retainers though at any time of her widowhood one of her deceased husbands brothers or cousins on his mothers side can relieve her by takeing her to wife himself should he have a wife at the time it cannot be murmered at by any one as he is in duty naturally bound to raise seed to his brother and she at his option or disposal; or she can be relieved by the clan women after a consultation should they think her in a bad situation they very often before the expiration of her widowhood have compassion on her forlorn state and thence give her a comb to comb her hair, or some of them comb her hair for her, and invest her with such clothes and ornaments as those of which she was divested for her widowhood, after they have gone through this ceremony with her she is at liberty to marry who she pleases, but should she not await the formal relief of her retainers, but in contempt of their prerogative, take to combing of her hair or marry a husband, they can treat her inconstancy is this as in any other case of adultery should she do it before the expiration of four years or four Boosketahs, from the death of her husband; but if she marrys a man and elopes with him and eludes the vigilance of her retainers to the expiration of the ensuing anniversary of the new corn Crop then she is free of their constraint and can live with her husband without fear of punishment and her husband either by her flight or punishment, for or about him is inseparably bound to her, and he cannot be implicated in the crime of adultery with her all the crime being imputed to her lewd disposition and incontinency, the same constraint ceremony and restrictions is observed with the man should his wife die first ~

as I have made frequent mention of their celebrating the anniversary of the new Corn Crop, Called by them Boos ke tah as much as to say (sacred purifying) which is the only thing wherein I ever saw them act as tho they paid an adoration to the all supreme they seem even when they are preparing to go to the festival to solemnize their mind and actions as a devout person would to enter a church to worship, it is evident that originally it must have had a great weight even in their political movements, for it will after its celebration stop the proceedings against any offender where life and death is not concerned and stealing is not exempted, all other misdemeanors passses into Oblivion and a new score is begun for the ensuing festival ~ The cowassawdays holds a festival more than the rest of the nation as they annually celebrate the coming of the new crop of beans with the same ceremonies as they do the festival of corn ~ as I have made a small digression from the point in the order of their festival I shall proceed to it in as accurate a manner as I can by saying that when the head men of a town sees the town or public corn is full in the ear and fit for use they set a day and inform the towns people when the sacred festival is to commence before the day arrives they nominate some of their Emathlahs, (which word is gone at his biding) to boil their physic that they drink & wash with to purify themselves, and of their most respectable chiefs they nominate three to officiate in the duties of the time as sacred priests or doctors. They then send some of the Emathlahs, to gather a Bush that acts as a quick and powerful emetic They call it micco ho yau e jah it is a kings cathartic. They brake anough to last the festival out. The Bush is very

[p. 66[25]]

25

much like in appearace to the low myrtle Bush but bears no Berries. when The appointed festival day arrives all the town people put out their fires and repair to the town house or square when They commence the sacred festival. They have particular songs and dances for it. They dance during the festival with intervals. Their singers are generally some men of eminence invited as proficient singers of some other town and they take it as a mark of distinction to receive an invitation for that purpose ~ after all have congregated the Select men to boil physic and those nominated to officiate as sacred men make a fire out of the public way so that they may not be polluted by the touch of an unpurifyed person during their Strict penance as they account their person sacred during their sacred and purified office ~ they proceed to boil their a wo teach caw which is an emetic. after it is thoroughly boiled the three men selected for the sacred office, take it after it is put into large cooling pans of Clay manufactury and prepare it for drinking and washing with. each man takes a pan and sits it before him and commences the process of Cooling having his head covered over and a joint of a cane in his hand. during the time they each sing a song of requests and thanks in a low under voice to the giver or taker of breath called saw ga unisse. in every interval the singer sticks his cane joint into the pan of awo teach caw and blows the virtue of said song of requests into the pan of physic in a most solemn manner, so that there-with it might operate in good to them that drink thereof. it is a quick and rapid emetic and drunk for that purpose by all the men and mostly all the women wash their children with it; the Creek indians have no variation in their annual celebration of the new crop of corn haveing particular songs and dances for the festive purpose. the commemoration in every town holds two days in the minor village towns from their commencement excepted; they hold twenty four hours. The Tuckabatchee town being the metropolis of the nation has a variety of shew in their solemn feast. they hold it six days. it is attended always by a large congregation who resort there to see and be seen ~

[p. 66[26]]
26

In their six days of <u>Boos ke tah</u> in which time neither those set apart for doctor of physic, nor such as are appointed to shew the strict rule or penance necessary on the occasion, make use of any thing to eat or drink but, the consecrated emetic of which they take profusely every day of the festival. They neither speak to nor touch a woman during said time as such a procedure would inevitably ruin their thanksgiving song, and instead of a blessing incur destruction not only to him that does it but to the community at large, nor will they shake hands with nor touch an unpurified friend during the time of their officiating. The whole festival is conducted with a grave supersticious solemnity to the last day. on the last day they take out and exhibit the aforementioned six brass or breast plates. They are carried a round by three men, one in each hand in that days dances, with much supersticious awe. said plates are kept under the care of two men always, and after their exhibition in the dances they are laid in their depository, which is under the seats that upholds the mats that the kings sit on, in their part of the council square. it is said that three of said brass plates has sign of hierogliphics on them, whilst others say that they could trace Hebrew Characters in a circle in the central part of the three oval ones, as they are scoured and burnished every year before they are exhibited no doubt but the characters are nearly defaced. Their account traditionally how they came by them is that they were thrown on handed down by the giver or taker of breath viz. saw ga emisse with an assurance to them that so long as they used them undefiled in their festivals that no people could divest them of their festival ceremonies or Country. on the same day they exhibit their manner of attack in warfare. several effigies are brought and placed about in the square to be attacked in a hostile manner, by men appointed for the

[p. 66[27]]

purpose, who to shew their skill in comeing on their enemy by stealth come on the effigies with all imaginable caution as tho unpercieved by them as an enemy when they get near the Square they all at once raise the war scream and charge on them, shoot tomahawk and scalp them, and tho pursued by others they make their escape as they would in actual attack. as many have past their time fasting it is necessary to eat of the new corn, and as all things in their political life has a new begining, it is necessary to have new fire to cook their corn and other eatables so that morning four men are appointed to that duty. They each take a block with a small incision in it and a round stick and apply it in the indenture of the block and roll it to and fro in the palm of their hands until it takes fire by the friction. there is great expression of joy when the new fire is made. every family in the town and even adjacent towns people take the new fire home to cook with for that year ~

In the process of the festival at night mostly in

intervals for rest the young men are divested of their given name that they had from infancy, and invested with what is called a war name which name they go and are known by the rest of their life. it is done thus. previously to the ceremony of naming it is intimated to the young man that is to be named by one of the kings or warriors for either can give names the name that he is thereafter to assume and go by. when the time arrives for the ceremony one of the kings or warrriors rises from his seat and calls the name in a shrill long tone of voice. at the call the young man rises and picks up the war club or mallet calld. by them Attussa and goes forth to him, when he informs the new man that he is now named as other men and he now can assume the manners and customs of other men. he then puts a feather in his head. when that is done the new dubbed man raises his war club above his head starts a long whoop and runs round in a circle to where he started and when he stops he cries youh youh. from that he is ever after a man with a name ~ after the Boos ke tah it is known that all light offences is past into Oblivion ~

[p. 66[28]]
28

The strongest link in their political and social standing as a nation is in their clanship or families. by their observance of it they are so united that there is no part of the nation detached from the other But are all linked harmonised and consolidated as one large connected family for by their family prescribed rules there is no part of the nation but a man can find his clansmen or their connection. the nation consists of nine clans or families viz. The Wind The Bear The Panther The Bird The Polecat The fox The Potato The red Paint and the isfauna which is composed of many small ones ~ of all the clans the most numerous &

previledged is is the wind family who are admitted exclusively to raise with their sticks and embody their clanspeople three times to take satisfaction of an offender toward one of their family, that is for minor offences such as commiting adultery stealing &c. by one of another family, whereas should any of the other clans rise with their sticks and embody once and the offender escape them and they lay down their sticks they can embody no more. The Boos ke tah is a curb and restraint to the priviledge of the wind family, for if an offender escapes, after one of the wind family has raised his clansmen, and keep out of reach to the celebration of the Boos ke tah then in that case they are as one of the other clans obliged to withhold ~ all the clans in the nation take their family descent from the mother being of the same family of the mother, and can only take a part with that family. The Father and his clan or family are only the father family to the children as he and his clan or family have no legal say or interest in the childrens family concerns. all the men of the fathers clan or family are called their father. The women are generally called their grandmother. all the men of the mothers family older than themselves are their uncles being their mothers brothers. all of their own age and under are called their brothers, and all the old women of their mothers Clan are called grandmother or aunt. all grown women of the wind family are to be called grandmother by all the other families. all the Clans are connected as friends or some distant relation throughout the nation;

[p. 66[29]]

29th. 29

so as I related it is the strong link of their political existance a complete curb and cement to their ferocious and vindictive nature when irritated, though their implacable and revengeful passion cannot be mitigated by the interference of Clan or familyship, when one of another Clan if even by chance should kill one of their blood relations on the mothers side of family, their customary laws in this is similar to the law of the Jewish legislator in reference to the manslayer excepting the city of refuge, for their law is literally whoso sheddeth mans blood by man his blood must be shed ~

Time nor distance cannot palliate their revenge for Should the perpetrator make his escape one of his brothers or cousins on his mothers side is taken. one of his blood kindred or himself must atone for the one lost male for male and female for female. even accidents are frequently made a matter of atonement, as far for instance as to be on business for another person and be killed by their horse the employer or one of the brothers or cousins must atone with their life for the death. for this reason they say had it not been for him and his business the death would not have happened. such reasoning may seem Strange when ex-pressd. by a people possessing their predistinarian princi-ples and tenets. when they reflect on any bad accident or misfortune happening to them it is a solace and comfort to them that it was unavoidable as it was foreordained that such and such thing was to be at that Elapsed period.

I will narrate a circumstance that happened of a deplorable nature to the Singer tho at that time he was head chief of the creek nation. I bring it forward to manifest their true character for retaliation for the loss of one of their blood kindred, tho their principal chief was the victim of their national custom. about the year 1808 the Singer covertly agreed with Col. Hawkins the U. S. agent in confidence, that he would go under the specious pretense of hunting and explore the country on both sides of the Mississippi river and if he found a country that would suit the nation that he would exert his imfluence with the nation to effect a sale of their place of nativity by treety and remove the nation to the new country ~ according to the concerted plan, without his even letting his brothers know his designs who accompanied him in his hunting excursion he went and struck the Mississippi high up and crossd. over to the west side.

[p. 66[30]]
30.
They had been over there but a short time till they came on the camps of part of a tribe that ever were their mortal enemies. They soon made an attack on one of their camps. in the conflict the Singer lost one of his brothers. after the encounter with the Husaws they returned to the East side not thinking it safe to remain on the other (as there has been ever an interminable warefare of the original tribes residing on the east and west sides of the Mississippi river, it was with extreme and guarded caution that they approached the haunts of each other, and since their trade and intercourse with the white people where they buy similar stuff for clothing, and the similarity of the fashion of their dress makes it hardily possible for them to recognize one of their own tribe from another without a salutation, so it happened in this case, for as one of the Singers brothers was on his researches near the Mississippi river he saw an Indian a crossing his way and supposing him to be an enemy who had crossd. the river for mischief he shot him dead and on his approaching him to get his scalp he recognized him to be a Cussetaw town man and one of his own nation. he returned to his own camp and informed his brothers that he had unluckily killed a man of their own nation through a mistaken Idea that he was a (was sas sa for so they call all their enemies on the west of the Mississippi). The people

of the Cussetaw camp upon their man not returning to the camp at night concluded that it was certain some accident had befallen him, and went in search for him the next day, and in their researches came on the Singers camp, who was alone. he directly proceeded to recount to them the nature of the sad affair and that it purely happened by a mistake of his brother who supposed him to be a was sas sa who had crossd. the river for mischief and he would retalliate on him for the loss of his brother that they killd. The cussetaws appeared satisfied with his account and convinced that it happended through a mistake. he informd. them farther that his brother and camp people were gone in search of their camp to inform them of the particulars of the accident. after they had eaten with him they started back for

[p. 66[31]]
their camp. on their way they concluded that as their brother was actually slain and it was acknoledged by whom, and as the manslayer was out of the way who had wantonly spilt their brothers blood that it would be but right to retaliate on him for the deed by depriving him of his brother by the same means, so they finally concluded to return to the camp which they did and killd. the Singer for his brothers killing theirs, through a mistake so that it is uncertain to think of makeing an effectual reconciliation after spilling of their kindred blood as they term it, in the fluctuations of their mind if at any time they can reach the perpetrator ~ if the Singer after his examination of the new country had but a lived to return his representations of its superior excellency to their place of nativity, may have awakened a sense of emigration in the nation even at that distant period, but his death unfortunately will ever leave the matter in doubt ~

In narrating such parts of their history as I have

attained I shall merely narrate the circumstance and not attempt to be exact as to time in a chronological order, but make it a rule to be as concise in a miscellaneous manner as I can, and move on the road of truth in my rehearsals, of such information as I have obtained with as much perspicuity and precision as the nature of the case will admit, as I shall adduce only such information as recollection and Oral testimony can furnish. I shall in that obscure tract, try a commencement of their political career as far back as the american revolution when they took a decided part with Britain through the persuation of imfluential men among them when they were neutral, tho they were easily buoyed up on that part through pure friendship to the English for their kind and friendly treatment to them, without regarding or knowing the cause of contest between the British and and the colonies. I may further say that they were under the imfluence of the English agent residing a mong them who was sent specially from Scotland for to strengthen their attachment towards England. he was not negligent toward his destination at the momentous crisis but made use of his imfluence to irritate them against the U. S. in his endeavors and false representations he was timely assisted by the Scottish traders who resided in the nation. many of 'em were connected by interest and otherwise to Adam Tate the British agent. When the traders saw how wholly he was devoted to the cause he advoted this

[p. 66[32]]

in order to make their court to him with ease, and please themselves, had frequent English peace talks for the Indians and inflamed their passion against the U. S. by their falsities untill they made them determine on action. they are naturally warlike and easily persuaded to mischief or warlike enterprises so as was expected in the result the deluded Indians advocated the British cause in word and action instead of keeping a neutral station as policy and interest would wisely dictate to them at all times. They immediately in their frenzy submitted themselves to be led by John Golfin James Leslie and Chs. Weatherford to the enterprize of British assistance when besieged in Savannah and augusta. in repeling the assailants at both of the above sieges, there was no man evinced more activity and courage than the then ruling chief of the nation calld. the old Morter who resided in the Hillabee Town. in a night rencounter with Genl. Waynes division he was severely wounded in his trip down to try a relief of one of the sieges. on the first attack the Indians charged the lines so quick that they successfully entered the camp and put to rout the part of Infantry or front guard who opposed their way, who had only retreated to the main body of the army to reinforce. in the mean time the Indians supposing that they had won an entire victory they fell to plundering the camp. in the process of pillageing the camp they fell over a Puncheon of old rum and as it ever has been and is now an established maxim with them to believe in the wonder workings and cheerful glee of the delicious stimulant to some cause and effect, in their enthusiasm they concluded and that naturally enough that as they had taken the camp and atchieved an easy victory over the soldiers and thereby even taken their rum, that they had in right of conquest when aided by a craveing disposition if possible to drink it up, but their easy victory proved a mistake for Genl. Wayne was not so easily to be vanquished for he came on them with his division of Veterans about the time that they had got their minds absorbed in rum, and unwary and careless of an enemy or any thing else, to that degree that they had unguardedly divested themselves of their weapons in which situation though surprised in their turn, with the point of the bayonet they attempted to maintain an unequal contest with double their number which of course could not last long ~

[p. 66[33]]

for after standing the point of the bayonet a short while they broke through the enemy and pursued their way on to their friends as they first intended. it is notorious that all such creek Indians as have had any intercourse or transactions of any kind or magnitude with the British or their emissaries whether of importance or not were ever partial to them and favorable to their Interest for many old men of the present day, to a very late period would and does now expatiate on the candid honest and liberal disinterestedness of the British as friends to the Indians in their talks to them or in their dealings, and they seemingly remark with wrath the contrast between the latter and the americans that in the observance of and faith in their contracts with the Indians that the English dealt with equitable justice and candour; but the latter with deceit and self interested political views that they ever make liberal promises to attain their purpose and only perform such parts of their contracts as will suit their convenience and evince thereby a faint recollection of the circumstance that was material to the cause ~

From the above stated oppinion of the american character the general disposition of the Creek tribe was rancorous and undoubtedly very unfavorable to the United States from the close of the revolutionary war to about the year of seventeen Hund. and ninety four when President Washington very humanely requested Genl. McGilveray a part Indian who was equally friendly to both parties to take a number of the imfluential chiefs of the nation to the seat of Govorment then in the city of Philadelphia which he accordingly did. The kind reception that was given the party by the President and cabinet was flattering being unused to the like, from white people, the paternal kindness and concern that was expressd. for their welfare by the President, made them reverence in his person their amiable great father and well wisher, and it was through him and his clemency displayd. towards them that acted as the incentive or cause why they returned to their homes effectually reconciled to the U. S. They related with exaggerated eulogy on their return how they had been received with kindness and hospitality and entertained by their great father Washington and how he had at different times instructed and admonished them to pursue the ways of peace and

[p. 66[34]]
34
amity with all the Indian tribes, and more especially with the U. S. in whose limits they resided and as neighbors of course they were mutually bound to blend their interests inseparably in all cases and more especially to cultivate their lasting friendship, for as they lived on one continent they were detached by the ocean from the feuds and interests of the powers of Europe; they said they could see and understand the propriety of his reasoning and to said pacific counsel the chiefs attended minutely, and on their return home, in their grand national council, they gave a detailed account of their talks and interviews with the great beloved man with a rehearsal of the good counsel he had given them, and the consideration and the due regard that they had for said counsel manifesting uncontrovertably the benefit and Utility they were confident that would ultimately result by the nation adopting and stedfastly pursuing said pacific principles ~ many still adherered to the wise and salutary advice of their great and adored father Washington when Tecumseh the earth-quake and spaniards all in

succession like the pandora Box made them waver. The first alarmed them in mind with the expectation of some dreadful event by a repetition of his prophetic problems. The second filld. them with awful expectations by its being unprecedented and unaccountable to them. The third by timeserving talks and observations, which ultimately caused such a distraction in the nation as made the majority without thought or hesitation enter into the ruthless war in the year Eighteen Hundred and Thirteen not only among themselves but against the U. S. which eventually nearly exterminated their nation, and circumscribed their once extensive country to the late ceded limits ~

In accord with the Presidents advice, given to the aforesaid chiefs they on their return home exerted their aid and imfluence in assisting Capt. John Chisholm who had humanely undertaken to reconcile a war between them and the Chickasaw tribe, pending for near a year. The Creek tribe had commenced hostilities on some frivolous grounds of misunderstanding with the former ~ They wage war thus. The national council is convened, and the nature of the offence,

[p. 66[35]]

35

is examined in a council of head Chiefs and Warriors and if they conclude that the cause of Collision is of so glaring a nature as to admit of no compromise or palliation, of nothing but the blood of the Enemy it is a positive declaration of war. The final conclusion of the chiefs is anounced to the assembled body of the Chiefs and Warriors by the orator explaining to them and the assembly the reasons why they are justified in a declaration of war. before they make a descent on their enemy, on a day appointed they assemble at their town house square in complete armour all stript and painted red black and white as they go into action with their guns on their shoulders their knife and tomahawk hanging to their side and war club stuck in their belt (a war club is shaped like a small gun about two foot long and at the curve near where the lock would be is a three square piece of iron or steele with a sharp edge drove in to leave a projection of about two inches). They all take their seats as they come. when assembled the man who is honored to be the town leader rises and takes his stand in the square when he raises the sacred war whoop and begins to sing & dance in the circle and as the rest rise they raise the same whoop and drop in behind the other. in a very little time their singing and dancing, is drowned by one eternal whooping and firing of guns ~ when they are assembled on their way to their enemy at the appointed rendezvouz they hold a general war dance in the same way as described above ~ I will try to return to the former subject. after a declaration of war and before they commence hostilities they proceed to gathering every man woman & child belonging to the nation to their respective town and relatives, let them be far or near. after they have collected all their kindred, they are ready to commence hostilities on the enemy. then if one of the other nation is seen by them he is certainly destroyed. their petty wars are wars of extermination. they commence by small parties on venture not man against man but tribe against tribe. it is a praise worthy action for a man or party of men to kill the women and children of their enemy, more so than to kill a man who is frequently in the forest, whereas to kill a woman shews evidently that he was not afraid to go into his enemys. Country but atchieved the manly deed in their very house door and escaped ~

[p. 66[36]]

The high opinion and self importance the creeks

had of of themselves, infered from their numbers and prowess; was their incentice to war on the other nation; in their wish to convince the chickasaws thereof in the summer of the year 1793 they made an irruption into their country with a collected force of near a thousand warriors headed by different chiefs but all headed and under the guidance of the Mad-dog of Tuckabatchee called Efau hadjo And Tobe of Talladega a man of a desperate character and ill repute. with them they associated as counseller James Leslie an old Scottish trader who headed them near the close of the revolution to assist the besieged in savannah. they used such precaution and dispatch in their descent on their enemy that it was not known that an invasion of their country was intended untill the firing announced their arrival. When they entered the enemies country they made Straight for a fortress built by William Colbert and his brothers for the safety of their families and dependants. they made an assault on the fortress which they could have taken on the first onset had they acted with a determined attack to enter it, but they commenced their firing and frightfull yelling at a considerable distance from the fort. The Chickasaws in the neighberhood on hearing the report of the guns mounted their Horses and made for the Fort but by a mistake made their way into the Creek forces, where they soon found that they were mistaken by five of them being instantly killed. The rest of them made their way safe into the fort. Thereafter the creeks took an unaccountable alarm for which they could not account and quit their attack of the fort with precipitation, and fled simultaneously for life as if danger was near. their flight was so intense and their panic so great all entreaty was unavailing, for Leslie and many of their mounted chiefs gained their front and used commands and expostulations to stop and rally them to a fight, but all was to no purpose.

They kept on in the same strain of runing, though they out numbered their pursuers by fifty to one. in their flight woe to the hindmost, for their pursuers for many miles selected and killed the most convenient of them without resistance. their panic caused their irretrievable overthrow.

[p. 66[37]]

37th 37

When they made their attack on Colberts fort it was tenanted only by them and their Connection not exceeding seven men and families besides a few negros with the addition of them that broke through the creeks force at the commencement of the attack made an aggregate number of seventeen men who and a few negros vanquished the Creek armament of near a thousant warriors, and killed and wounded near a hundred of them. This defeat terminated the active operations of their war with the chickasaws, and served greatly to humble the pride of the Ispocogas. Shortly after the rencounter capt. J. Chisholm with the assistance of others, and the chiefs of the tribes, mediated a pacific treaty between them which has been unalterable ever since.

About the same time they carried on a marauding and predatory war-fare with the new setlers of Cumberland river in the state of Tennessee who they alledged were a trespassing on their ground, that they had and were opening and inhabiting plantations in their principal hunting ground, that said portion of the forest had fell to their lot, in their partition of hunting ground with the other tribes, as such it was their opinion that they had a right to retain that portion of the forest unsullied and undefiled by the touch of the axe or plow. They apprehended rightly that so long as the forests retained their primary uncultivated state from the proceeds of the game killed therein that is from the sale and

Barter of their peltry they clothed themselves and families, and got their winter supply of meat independant of labour; but if it was settled by the white people and plantations opened in it of course such a support must fail entirely; & be succeeded by a general want of such supplies natural and artificial ~ At that time their place of trade and barter centered in Pensacola a small Spanish town in Florida where there was established a large commercial house under the firm of Panton Leslie & Co. who engrossd. the Entire trade of the adjacent national tribes by a barter of groceries and goods for their peltry and furrs. Through the channel of white traders who were located in the nation, for the purpose of trade, said traders through interested motives, misadvised them and by false representations irritated their passions to make reprisals for supposed injuries that would be, they induced them eventually to commit murders among the recent Settlers of Tennessee and Steal their horses, under the impressed idea that such a procedure ~

[p. 66[38]]

38

would deter the white people from moveing into the country, and thereby they could do their hunting undisturbed. The dishonest part of the traders urged them on and instigated their stealing of the horses from the Tennesseans which horses when Stolen they bought for four or five gallons of rum, to pack their peltry and hides on to market. after the furr and peltry trade was put down in Europe and packing of horses to market of no farther use, the stealing of horses was so prevalent a habit with the white and red man, that they followed it, but in a lighter passion to the war of Eighteen hundred and thirteen ~

The Indians in their primary nature even at this day are disinterestedly honest though indolent and negligent to a blameable degree, but they apologise for their habitual defects now by asserting that before their innate passions and morals were corrupted by the white men residing among and those having an intercourse with them, that stealing from each other was unknown to them, being raised poor and habituated to that life that they felt no anxiety for the goods or property of another, so they had no excitement to perpetrate acts of thievery for the acquisition of a thing that they did not crave nor know the want of ~ It is a hard case for them that their first visitors were a debauched indolent dishonest set, without the fear of man or God and only afraid of labour. had they been visited by a pious industrious Virtuous set of men and they had admitted them to locate among them and inculcate examples and instructions of piety, labour and virtuous pursuits, from them, instead of the first impressions of vice and impiety their case at this day would have been far different, and it would have saved a great effusion of innocent blood that has flown with profusion. Many a father would not have lamented the children swept from under his care under shocking circumstances nor the orphan the father and protector of its tender years ~ many on both sides would have had no cause but to be a careless friend to the other side, in the same bosom that has cause and reason to call for retribution and revenge, all the above emanating from the ill examples and worse advice of a few men fit only for the dregs of any society ~ It is remarkable that the creeks in all trials and meandering Scences of their political life, have had a true magnetic predilection for the British, for they would declare without reserve at a very late date their adherence to them as friends and as unresedly express their abhorrence of the virginians as they term the americans, and at this or any other period if they had an intercourse with the British their partiality would recur and manifest and evince itself by some frenzied movement, so great is their infatuation for to incur the English favour ~

The last notable effort they made in the american revolution to serve their friends was near the close of it, by a feeble attempt they made to succour their British and tory friends when besieged in Mobile by Don Galves and the Choctaws who repaired to his standard. The creeks raised and embodied about two hundred warriors in order if possible to raise the siege. They repaired to the place of contest headed by the old morter of the Hillabee town under the persuasion of raising the siege on their arrival. They went down on the east side of the Alabama river under the guidance of Richard T. Coleman a Georgian by birth, untill they reached a Bluff immediately above the town of Blakely east of Mobile, where they encamped expecting to be immediately transported by their friends over to Mobile. They did not know that their friends was debarred of egression, but their arrival and purpose being known to the Spaniards and Choctaws first, their friends in Fort Charlotte were anticipated in crossing over to give them a visit of Welcome to their shore, for the choctaw force and a few Spaniards crossed over the Bay, and nearly surprised them with about an equal force. the Old Morter and his men though taken unaware were not daunted but returned the war whoop and met their assailants with manly courage and worsted them in the onset, but the Choctaws turned the scale by an act of desperation which is common to them when hard run in battle that is by throwing aside their fire arms and makeing an effectual attack, with their tomahawk and scalping knife in hand. The ispocogas unused to so close a combat in repeling their foe, gave ground with precipitation in all quarters, and left their leader with a few others in an unequal contest which could not last doubtful long as they were generally wounded. The Ispocagas lost of their force upwards of fifty warriors. of their wounded but a few escaped, for they mostly graced the scalp pole of the choctaws. The Old Morter effected his escape out of battle though mortally wounded of which he died the next day on the road about twenty five miles above his last Battle ground for his British friends. This was about the last scene of warfare in the eventful revolution of N. America ~

[p. 66[40]]
40

after the close of the american revolution the Creeks still lived under the controul of their own institutes unconnected with the events of any but their own nation till about the year of seventeen hund. and ninety eight the U. S. Govorment located an agent among them. their first agent was col. Benjamin Hawkins from Indian Eulogy he was a Gentleman qualified to fill the trust reposed in him with reputation and rectitude. the Indians in their first transactions with him, were very distrustful of him and his office. they held frequent debates among themselves on the propriety of the idea they had in contemplation of killing him. they thought that he was merely imposed on them by the Govorment as a Spy and a snare to shackle their liberties, but in their meetings and consultations with him in an official way, they could not but admire his firm candid and honest deportment. The more they became acquainted with him the more they were reconciled to his office among them. They loved him for his virtuous and disinterested greatness of mind, for he expressd. to them his hopes and wish for their welfare ~ he took pains to learn their language in which he was very fluent. in a little time by his own counsel he tamed the wild savage and by personal ensample and instruction he made a farmer and husbandman of him. he taught and familiarized him to the sound of the Blacksmiths anvil and the weavers batton, for when he located among them there did not exceed in the whole nation a half dozen fences made of rails. their fencing consisted of forks about two feet high and cross staked and poles laid in the crosses to the height they intended their fence to be. They disused their antient manner of fences with forks and poles and by noticeing his farm and plantation as an example for their instruction many of them soon fenced with rails and enlarged their farms, and not two of them in fifty had seen the process of spining and weaveing in which branches and other domestic arts by his individual reasoning example and encoragement, he so far improved them in domestic pursuits of life, to the time of the war of 1813, that they were far more edified in domestic arts industry and civilization than at this day. it is a case to be regretted that he did not live to see the shew and enjoy the emanative result of his progressive improvement among them, and it is as lamentable that his virtuous high and disinterested mind did not succeed within the intention and body of his successors in office as well as in their persons, for the principal

[p. 66[41]]

41

Aim of his successors has been to devise ways and means to withhold from the Indians as much of the Stipend covertly as possible in instances nearly all, without once condescending to admonish or instruct the poor unthoughted wretches in the sober habits or domestic pursuits of life. Col. Hawkins by his unwearied exertions in moral precepts somewhat smoothed the rough and ferocious son of nature and man of the forest. for the want of such a guide, observe on the contrary; by the designed neglect of his successors in not giving wanted good counsel, to induce them thereby to quit their froward practices, and pusue the paths of rectitude and occupy their minds beneficially as their circumstances required. time has seen them slide down the declivity of degradation to the lowest verge, a set of perfect and consumate sots, a circumstance much lamented by the few sober and thinking kind of them. after they had convinced themselves by strict observation of Col. Hawkins conduct, they made sure that his counsel was intended for an individual and national benefit the Chiefs gradually placed their confidence in him seeing his upright conduct and integrity, and counted their national affairs safe under his management untill about the year 1812 when their confidence was put to the Test. some two or three cos-awdas previous to that date accompanied some seminolas of the Shawanase tribe who went to see their progenitors on the waubash about the time the Shawanose prophet began to propagate a belief among the northern tribes of Indians of his wonder workings, and inspired knowledge of future events. The cowasadas protracted their visit long anough in that country to imbibe his notions of the whitemans oppres-sive and domineering encroachments on indian rights. they returned for home with different ideas and opinions to what they carried there with them. they were fully lectured and convinced of all the overbearing wrongs they had and were likely to experience and suffer, and no doubt of the success-ful revenge the Indians would have in exterminating the white people before long, for dispossessing them wantonly and insatiably of their lands and country contrary to order purposed by the creator and that he in his wrath would assist the Indians in the recovery of their lands and country, which he had made on purpose for their special use and suited it for 'em in fruits of all kinds acorn trees & Spontaneously bearing eatables for their subsistance of nature and comfort of life. such lectures he avowed in a prophetic manner. The principal of the Cawasadas was named Taskeegee Tustonuggee or for Common Ho co lee which is two in their tongue. on their way home they could not forego the impression

[p. 66[42]]
42
imbibed of the prophet for in the State of Tennessee they commited some outrageous murders on some unoffending families for no other provocation than being white a people doomed in a short time to come, for Indian destruction according to the prophets prediction, of the will of the great maker of all things. about the time of the grand Creek national council being convened the murderers divulged the secret by vaunting of the deed and giveing themselves great merit for the act they had perpetrated it being according to the undeviating pleasure of God. at the same time the case was urged on the national council by by the agent of the U. S. for satisfaction. Therefore Ho co lee and the others concerned in the murders were convicted of the crime by the grand national council on the evidence of their own report and slain on the spot. at this time of times and events the whole nation began to be frenzied and looked out daily in expectation of a phenomena or event of a direful nature, occasioned by occurrencies that they had not comprehension to understand the nature of. they thought to attain a solution of the mystery by enquiring the cause of each other, but their enquiries only made the case more involved

in blind conjecture so they were ripe in fanatical frenzy, to imbibe Tecumsehs mad notions that he avowed on his visit to them in his public speech to the assembled body of the nation, when they gave him audience. what heightened their astonishment into almost a certainty, was a coincidence of Tecumsehs omenous remark in his public speech to The shock of the earth quake, and the appearance of the comet previous. on its forebodings of ill to their enemies he commented in an alarming manner. two such uncommon Occurrencies in succession aided with his comments occasioned the fabrication of the most dreadful tales to impress a weak mind with a belief of something to happen, not common in the course of nature. said flying tales daily multiplyed and were exaggerated in all parts of the nation, told and recived as truth by every one. all their foolish tales had no Father for they were said to be told by first one and then another and no body could ascertain who, but the relators were at a distance ingeneral and hard to be detected. moreover their ill fated destiny prepared their minds to recieve as evident truth all Tecumsehs fanatical Tales. his visit was previous to the national council long anough for him to inform them Thoroughly of his views on the pending conflict that he meditated to have with the americans, and prepossess them in his favour ~

[p. 66[43]]
Though they are the most obsequious of all subjects to their laws and head men, but at that time they threw off all restraint, and oppenly arraigned the justice of their chiefs in the tranaction of their haveing the aforesaid murderers killed, in their then situation of mind they were prepared for any following occurrence let the same be as it would, for their minds was in an uproar for mischief ~ during Tecumsehs stay he tried all the rhetoric he was master of, to

induce the Big Warrior the then head of the national chiefs and the subordinate chiefs to sanction the project and join in his plan for an Indian league. The plan was for all the Indian tribes on the continent to hold their lands in one common stock, and no sale of any of their lands to be valid only by the consent being first obtained of all the tribes. on Tecumsehs first arrival the Big Warrior and capt. Isaacs attended to his peace talk and accepted the calumet and Tobacco and smoked friendship with him. They learnd. his new war songs and dances. The novelty of the new war dances Brought them in vogue. it appears that capt. Isaacs had apprehended or contemplated a thing of the kind before this period, for he had gone, the summer preceding to Mobile and bought fifty bags of powder. he was so far in a condition and preparation for war, if such a thing as war was in mind among them it never was divulged to this day. Tecumsehs new war songs and dances, was sung and danced in all the towns on the Tallapoosy before the grand national council was convened, but not generally known that there was any thought of or preparation for a war, or such a thing in contemplation, for very few were in the secret, and those to whom it was intimated and knew it, was such as were known to be so minded both in principle and inclination. Tecumseh had said to many in private and repeated it to the national council in audience, his fixed determination to war with the americans. he stated to them the great supernatural powers he possessed. he said if he was to beat the white people in his intended conflict with them and obtain his desire, they would know it by the following sign, that he would ascend to the top of a high mountain in about four moons from that time

And there he would whoop three unbounded loud whoops slap his hands together three times and raise up his foot and stamp it on the earth three times and by these actions call forth his power and thereby make the whole earth tremble which would be omenous of his success in the undertaking. if such did not happen they would know that he was to fail in the enterprise. This and many more speeches that he made of a miraculous nature did not lessen his reputation but exalted him in the estimation of the majority of the nation. They looked on him as superior eminent and one of the most consumate and fearless warriors of his time and a man worthy of imitation ~ When Col. Hawkins attended the grand Creek national Council he expressed to them his surprise to see their abject and imbecile state and that he was sorry to see them so weak minded as to be led astray and attempt desperate measures so as thereby endanger the safety of themselves and nation if persisted in, that they were infatuated by studied tales fabricated to suit their understanding and manners, and to fathom their propensities, and put forth to beguile them, and would result ultimately in their ruin. The words of reason flowing from their beloved man, did not find then all like Festus of old deaf to the words of truth and soberness, for in the Big warrior the found a light of returning reason; he acknowledged his & their folly and said, that he saw plainly that it was easier to begin an interruption than to end one. he knew that the power and resources, of the tribes together was no match for the americans. he said he saw farther, that an Indian league would be but a weak cord to effectually unite their Interests in their detached situation, and that on the whole, it was but a frenzied undertaking without a solid foundation and must fall inevitably with its own weakness. He then in order to establish his peaceable disposition on its former standing in Col. Hawkins's mind and make an atonement for his past folly advised the killing of Tecumseh, as a propagator of mischief among them, thinking the time, the place and public execution of him, with a full explanation of the reason of such a treatment of him, would stop the mad proceedings in agitation among the thoughtless, and cool the lukewarm, and favorably establish the wavering minds of many ~

[p. 66[45]]

45

But when he expressed his opinion of what he thought of doing to Tecumseh in their council house, it was shocking to many of his adhereing chiefs. They said the perpetration of such a deed seemed wrong and unprecedented to them. by such a deed they must lose the faith of all nations, as he Tecumseh had come to them in token and reliance of a friendly man to a friendly nation, and had done nothing to them worthy of death, that their voice and advice was that he and his talks might go away in peace as he came, which would keep them clear of his blood. after he had diseminated his malevolent and corrosive imaginations of mind in the breast of many he took his leave of them to see if he could infuse mischief in the other tribes. As his calm and determined manner and independence was the admiration of the Ispocoga tribe, they could not but venerate his prophetic manner of delivering his speeches, which he did without any seeming doubt of their accomplishment. what he said, he infered was afore dictated to him by the great spirit, of whose will and mandates he acted as the mere organ, by which he proselyted many who thought his singular manner of relating omens and predictions worthy of imitation. so the age and time of prophecy in the creek nation, preceded the light of reason and knowledge for a time. many turned prophet which was a prelude to all the mad and diabolical actions that could be thought of, or performed and all attributed to inspiration. They improved in folly so far as to pretend to have frequent and long conversations with the great master of breath upon different topics relative to the future. these pretended dialogues soon became a matter of destruction to many of the well meaning and peacefull part of the people, for a man to intimate or express the least doubt of their being inspired, or say he doubted the truth of their auguries he was sure to be a victim of a prophetic wrath. by such harsh purifying they soon silenced and humbled the opposition, and by expatiating always on the certainty of destruction that would befall the unbeliever and incorrigible for their untoward conduct, they made the community at large, subservient by degrees to the prophetic mandates, whether they believed in them or not. in their prophetic incantations they could be assured of such as were witches and dealt with evil disposed spirits. The people generally would believe such a report, as they Are tinctured with Superstition and believe any thing of a marvelous report, so as soon as

[p. 66[46]]
46
a man was announced to be acquainted with the work and dismal effect of the diabolical art, such as flying about the country far and near, to poison such people as were inimical to them, or blow and infuse a contagious air into a house, in passing by it at night or into the nostrils and lungs of a particular person when asleep by which they very often destroyed by instant death, a person or whole of a family that they did not like, they were then said to be seen at twilight ... of an evening a flying about to do mischief,

whenever such a person was found, it was not for him to exculpate himself. he was siezed by a mob tied to a tree with ropes and lightwood piled around him set on fire and he burned to death with as little compunction or remorse of conscience, as in the Roman inquisition. many of the most enlightened and well disposed to peace and good order among them, were brought to a fiery ordeal for the common good. all this was done that the fanatics and evil disposed might bear the sway and reign undisturbed and no counsel was tolerated or adduced before the public, but such as suited the disposition of the times. in the commencement of their wild sallies of pretended and deceptive inspiration Capt. Isaacs bore a very conspicuous part, in the catalogue of inspired men, & bore the palm for a while from his contemporaties. he began as a conjuror first, in which art he soon became eminent by representing his skill and knowledge in the art of enchantment, as unequalled that was he so minded he could and would petrify any one that opposed and thwarted his measures in any way. he was continually relating, the wonderful things he could do and the miraculous things he had done. one thing was of his diving down to the bottom of the river and laying there and traveling about for many days and nights recieving instuction and information from an enormous and friendly serpant that dwels there and was acquainted with future events and all other things necessary for a man to know in this life. by such tales his art was dreaded and by the foolish herd his person held in superstitious veneration. he with all the other divine pretenders were induced to pretend their wonder workings, from Tecumsehs public speech coinciding or happening so near in time to the first shock of the earth quake, which happened about three moons from the time of Tecumsehs speech, instead of four moons that he said would elapse before he manifested his omenous power, and by it let them know the future events of his meditated war ~

[p. 66[47]]

as their minds were in a ferment and they solicitous to know for what, an event occurred to quiet their incertitude. The earthquake happening so near the time that Tecumseh was to convince them of his power and truth, by his actions on the mountain to shake our globe, they were certain that the shaking was done by him. Their conviction of the event left no room to doubt any thing he had said of the successful irruption of the Indians against the white people. after being uncontrovertably convinced of their success they thought it an act of madness not to wage and prosecute a war that portended success to their undertakings which was to expell the white people from their lands and rightful country according as willed and directed by the great master of breath ~ When they first began their fanatical iruptions, and preparations for a social and general war, the big Warrior was apprehensive of a storm in such a cloud of incidents and seeing them on the progressive order from bad to worse, he thought it adviseable to fortify himself and adherents in Tuckabatchee and be in readiness for them in any hostile movement that they might make against him, for he expected they would attempt to do something against him as he was a dissenter from their plans of war operations, for they indicated from their movements to be ripe for innovation, for about the same time that he commenced fortifying and previous to it, the adjacent towns people had assembled at othlewallee or cluwallee above the mouth of line creek and began an entrenched camp, and the Whole nation was in commotion and excited, and not one of them could tell for why, or account for what purpose. all the information they could collect or hear by assembling or inquiring of each other was that the ferment and agitation was almost a general thing and superlatively progressing from bad to worse, by and through the prophetic men, who were daily augmenting and as their number increased, they vied with each other who could excell in wild predictions and who would adduce the most romantic circumstances of a frivolous nature to confirm it a divine call. They atlength got emulous who could have the most various prophetic missions, that is circulating reports of their frequent interviews and familiarity with the great giver or taker of breath and by such reports raise their fame so as thereby they could gain the ascendancy over the multitude and awe them into a submission to their will. as an instance of the foregoing plan and in order to awe the people, Josiah Francis a half blooded Frenchman, who was of the prophets, received an order from the master of breath, to meet him every day at a certain

[p. 66[48]]
48
place, as he intended to teach him the different languages that he would want to Use, and writing so as he would be enabled to transact his own and the national affairs without applying for such assistance from another person. according to the divine injunction, he absented himself every day as if he attended for his tuition, which many believed to be the case. in a short time he informed his adherents that he was leearned in the branches of writing and languages perfect enough to converse write and do his own business. The next thing was to convince them of the fact of such a miracle by shewing Them of it. That his divine favour might never more be doubted, he wrote a lengthy letter in

spanish (of which language he know not a word) to the Govr. of Pensacola requesting him in it, to send to him arms and ammunition of which articles he stood in great need, to carry on hostilities agains the americans. he give his envoys a circumstantial and full detail of the contents of his letter, by reading and interpreting the substance of it to them in a precise manner; (in their way of ridiculing his presumption, they have said since that his letter looked more like a paper full of crooked marks than writing.) They carried it nevertheless, to the Govr. as they had to do without an audible remark, for fear of their lives. When the Govr. received and opened the letter and asked them the reason why such a paper of marks was sent to him, their opinion of the legible writing of it, was verified, for he declared to them in the positive that it contained not a letter of writing. they saw that he was angry about it and wished to exculpate themselves from the imputation of passing a slur on him by giveing him such a paper. They satisfied him on the above heads by detailing to him all that Francis said was contained in the letter. The Govr. seeing their simplicity had no doubt of their innocency in the case, and that they were imposed on, and probably knew nothing of the deception practised on them. when they finished relating to him all francis's mad deeds and sayings, he laughed heartily, and jocosely ridiculed Francis for pretending to write, and said he had a notion to return him a letter in answer of the same unintelligible writing informing him, that he had no arms nor munitions of war for him. so they returned home without arms or ammunition ~

[p. 66[49]]

49

Josiah Franciss and Paddy Walsh seeing themselves put fairly in the back grounds by the riseing fame of Capt.

Isaacs felt emulous and coleagueed to rival and cast him down from the pinnacle of his fame, so that after his fall they might retain between them an entire ascendancy over the multitude, who they intended to domineer over by prophet craft. as a begining to his downfall they pretended a divine information that Isaacs in his conjurations and ominous revelations got his information from a familiar diabolical spirit who had moreover taught him a singular way of diveing in the water and flying through the air for mischivous purposes, that he had power to injure and destroy any one that he pleased, provided they did not use salt victuals, that there was different disposed witches some of good and others of bad towards mankind that Isaacs's friend was of the latter class, so he was pronounced a diabolical witch beyond any doubts. The community proscribed him, and his portion was to be death by fire, to cleanse his body of the pollution that was attached to him through his wicked practices. There was some of his adherents truly attached to him and that so reverendly that they resolved to share his precarious fortunes with him. They soon let him know his impending fate it taking and of the great defection in his party, and after they held a consultation of what to do, to ensure his and their safety they decamped with the determination to put themselves at the mercy of the Tuckabatchees who they expected more consistant than those they were about to leave. accordingly they joind. their Interests with the Big Warrior in his fort with a full resolve to share both good and bad fortune with the Tuckabatchians. it was an unfortunate circumstance for the Hostile camps that when Isaacs made his moveing flight that he did not forget his powder and lead, that he had on hand, but was mindfull to carry it with him, thinking it would make him welcome with his new party that heretofore had no friendship with him. in this calculation he was not mistaken as they were very much in want of powder and lead. Therefore his arrival with ammunition and a reinforement of Tuskeegee and cawassada fugitives was hailed with a hearty welcome, And both his return to reason and defection from his late friends was highly extolld. The scare that Capt. Isaacs got in the camps of his late party which caused his precipitate flight to the Big warrior was what saved the Tuckabatchians, first the acqusition of his powder and lead of which they were too scant for a siege or Battle secondly

[p. 66[50]]
50
the reinforcement brought by him which give the fort more strength by augmenting their force to six hundred effective men for war. it never was ascertaind what the force of the hostile camp was, as there never was a time when all was in camp at once, but the hostile band was four thousand eight hundred, a dreadful odds to be in eight miles of each others forces, in mortal enmity. The cautious flight that Capt. Isaacs made to save his life caused irritation and a great uproar in the hostile camp, that a witch known to be of the worst kind should escape their just vengeance. They collected their whole force and made an immediate and rapid attack on the Tuckabatchee fort, but were repulsed with considerable loss. They made an attack every day for some days and through their daily loss of men, without makeing an impression on the fort, they laid siege to it thinking to starve it to surrender. what made the hostiles so determined to take the Fortress was that they might once more have their fugitive witch in their power to torture him with fire and splinters of lightwood to death and recover the possession of the much needed powder. it was soon known over the whole nation that the hostile attacks on the Big

Warriors fort was turned to a siege. when the cowetaws of Chattahachee found out the true situation of the Tucka-batchees they sent a large force to their relief under the controul of Joseph Marshall, who went into the fort through the river line of the hostile camps. The second day after the entry of the reinforcement, the hostile band came to a conclusion to make another and final effort on the fort, to crush the opposing party at a blow. Quite early in the day they made an assault simultaneously up to the very pickets where they were recieved in so deadly a manner that many of them to escape being killed laid down as tho' they were dead whilst a braver class laid down and roled over to the pickets and tried to cut them down, but after an assault supported for some time by emulation and mortal hatred they made a retreat but not as men beaten off but daring the besieged to follow them. They must have felt themselves roughly handled for the Big Warrior and marshall the next day started for the State of Georgia. The women and children mixed with armed men marched out of the fort in a line for the river and crossed it for Georgia and followd.

[p. 66[51]]

51

Closely by all the men in their Rear, stript to their naked bodies and painted red black or white ready and willing to fight for their wives and children. Their determined manner must have damped the ardour of the hostiles for they never pretended to molest 'em in their comeing out of the fort nor pursue them on the road, so they had no interruption on their escape into Georgia. in the aforesaid assault on the fort J. Marshall lost one of his eyes by a bullet touching his eye ball. I never could find any that even conjectured what the killed and lost of the two parties could be. But I would suppose the loss of the hostile party considerable by the Big warriors easy escape. had they not a been considerably cripled they would have made one more attempt to capture Capt. Isaacs ~ So ended this siege that caused the Big-warrior to abandon the nation to the hostile band, first instigated by the fanatical and self made prophet and upheld by the deluded multitude. This was the commencement of that civil and general war which they prosecuted in ruthless manner for no cause, untill they devastated the creek or ispocaga tribe ~ it may be observed that from the afore-said period, the result of all their undertakings manifestly shews, that misfortune had selected them for her darling and nurtured them in scenes of misguided afflictions, and destined them to seal their fate however disapproved by them in the wild forests of the west, after being the Thor-oughfare of every series of practical villany; that ever was heard or thought of before or to be hereafter ~ When the Big warrior was rescued (from the precarious situation in which he was placed) by Marshall and the cowetaws, and when he quit and gave up the nation to the hostile party and took shelter in the state of Georgia it was plain that the die was cast, and nothing could turn up but a civil and a general war to terminate their differences and establish their different views; as yet some had only contemplated to effect the destruction of the Big-warrior, Capt. Isaacs and their party, whilst others were for pillage and war on all that opposed their way, whitemen or Indians. The latter opinion preponderated the first, and the entrenchments of the hostile camp was enlarged and extended so as to embrace two parts of the Othlewallee that is both sides of the Tallapoosy river near the mouth of line creek ~ while they stayed in said camps they felt a freedom and wished to live plentifull on beef, as the stock holders were mostly gone, they wantonly killed all the cattle in nation and negligently wasted the meat, that would have supported them many months with economy and a little care. by their extravagance in living they soon came to want of provisions and near starvation while their camps were in a state of plenty. it was the continual resort of the hostile band, for all others were interdicted by a say of the prophecyers. They pretended that a man of a contrary opinion could not impose himself on them, for they could tell a man who was opposed to their measures, so quick as they touchd. any part of him, or a man that eat salt victuals, for on shakeing hands with any man of the description aforesaid the prophet instantly commenced trembleing and the defilement subsided by a gradual jerking and working of all his muscles, not excepting his face, which jerking of his muscles concluded in a tremble of all his flesh. during the agitation he did not appear to labour under any strain to effect such a working of his nerves, but they certainly done it by a strain on the nerves, which he could effect by habitual practice ~ as war with all the attendant horrors was determined on, it was necessary to be prepared for the consequences, and as capt. Isaacs had eloped and saved himself from their vengeance, with his powder and lead and nearly left them destitute of the essential article, it was necessary to have some and that was to be procured from their spanish friends only in Pensacola, as that was the only place they dared to approach to get or buy any. as it was impossible for them to subsist or carry on war without powder and lead, there started for Pensacola in order to purchase some, or recieve it from the spaniards as a compliment, a body of two hundred and eighty men headed by their most persevereing prophetic man, called high headed Jim, and by them cussetaws Tusto nug gie, on the seventh of July Eighteen hund. and thirteen, as on their way down to Pensacola at burnt coin Springs they charged on the house of James Cornels and he not being at home they took Mrs. Cornels and a man called Marler and carried them on to Pensacola with them, and sold them there as prisoners of war to citizens of the place who give the Indians a small price to get them out of their possession. When they attacked Cornels house and took Mrs. Cornels their inroad into the country was so unexpected that they had it completely in their power to have made a general sweep of the country down to the present town of Stockton.

[p. 66[53]]

53

But fortunately for the country at that time it was saved by Indians miscalculating on an event. at their takeing Mrs. Cornels they were so intent in plundering the house that they never noticed a couple of negros about the place who directly run off towards the river settlement about fifteen miles from there. when they recalled them near an hour after, they sent in pursuit of them to the next house, where they were all gone. Then they were sure that that man would speed to the river and give an alarm before they could reach there in pursuit with a force sufficient to do any thing of account. It proved otherwise than was calculated for him to do, for when the runing negro's told him of the Indian descent on the country, they done it thinking that he would make speed to inform the river settlement of their danger so that they might shift themselves out of danger, but he had no thought on the case. being an unthoughted Selfish being he cared for only his own safety. he mounted his small family on horseback and made into the woods for security. had the Indians continued their pursuit of the negros they would have overtaken them before they reached the next house, but the pursuers wanted the foreknowledge of their prophet in this case to regulate their pursuit with perseverance, so the negros give the alarm themselves. When they got to the next mans house, he was not so selfish nor carefull of his horses. all his thoughts was to warn his friends of their danger so that they might extricate themselves by a timely flight, which they did by his flying intelligence in a little time; immediately after Mrs. Cornels capture all those inhabiting the lower part of the state on the eastern bank both Indians and white people repaired with all their moveables to a place known as the cut off bordering and in the white settlement, wherein on a general consultation, the indian refugees and inhabitants of the place concluded on the propriety of fortifying against a future irruption of the hostile Indians and erected the ever memorable fort Mimbs. Near about the time that Fort Mimbs was completed in accordance with the opinion of the country James Callier the Colonel of the County as in duty bound mustered all the men he could numbering about one Hundred and Eighty men of part Indians and white men. The purpose of the expedition was if possible to meet the Indians that went to Pensacola for to procure ammunition on return from there with it, give them battle and take their

[p. 66[54]]

54

powder and lead if they should have any. The Col. and his guides made a circuitous rout without seeing any Indians and were nearly out of expectation of meeting any untill they arrived at a branch of burnt corn creek in conecah County. There they saw about a half dozen of them out of the Creek swamp. as quick as they could they charged on them and run them back to the swamp. a body of them of a 'bout sixty men was in the creek swamp where they were met by the flying party, and when they met and had painted themselves for battle they came out of the swamp and made a hideous and yelling attack on the Colonels assailing corps. though there was sixty men of the Indians they had but thirteen guns among them. The unarmed ones assissted during the action by whooping and encourageing the armed men which was all they could do in their circumstances. what few guns they had was enough it appeared to gain a decisive and almost bloodless victory for on their comeing out of the swamp with the charge and war whoop, the Colonels men were panic struck and made a rapid and quick retreat which soon became a flight and that so intensely that many never fired a gun. Tho' the Colonel sent some of his officers on fleet horses, to gain their front and remonstrate with them on their unmanly conduct and to return and fight in spite of all arguments to the contrary they kept on in the same speed. Their panic was greater than the honor of their country with them, at that time. The white people lost five men killed and as many wounded. among the latter Col. Samuel Dale got shot in one shoulder. The Indians lost two and a negro killed and five wounded. The negro was killed in makeing his escape from the Indians to the white people for their protection. The victory gained by the hostile party on their return to their camps, almost without haveing to fight in the event proved their own overthrow for it give them an exalted opinion of their own valour and prowess and a most contempable one of the americans who they were confident was touched by a cowardly spirit by the will of the master of breath, so that the Indians would have less trouble in destroying them, as such would be before long, almost without resistance it Being so preordained ~

when the Indian hostile troop found that their men who went in pursuit of the negros who run off from the sack of Cornels house, had returned without them, and reported that they were sure that the negros had alarmed the river settlement, of course the country would all be apprised of their intentions and inroad into the department, and they would be on the alert and ready to recieve them, and that their present trip was not to slay and fight their enemy, but their object was a supply of ammunition, of which article at this time they were in great need, so on this observation they proceeded on their first intent to Pensacola. when they got there they soon demanded an interview of the Governor, and Intendant, who at that time thought that themselves and town was in a critical situation, to have so few Soldiers to guard the town, at a time when near three hund. ferocious indians were in it, so intent for war that they made it an impertinent measure to beg or demand ammunition alternately, throwing out hints in an oblique way of what they might do in case they were compelled to act as a dernier resort. The Govr. gave them at length a private audience, but in it, it was never known if they concerted any plan of operations as the interpreter would never tell of such a thing. by some means unknown they got several horse loads of powder and lead which they carried off with them and they after this ever got their supplies of ammunition at that place, whether from the Govorment authorities or citizens it is unknown as I believe it was known to very few of either side, but I never doubted but there was a general concern made both by the authorities and citizens to sell or compliment them with as much ammunition as they wanted at all times when they called for it. before the Indians left Pensacola in order to go home, Coll. Calleir had calld. for volunteers in order to give them battle expressly to get their powder. at that time there was several men who were acquainted with many of the Indians, went down to where they were in Pensacola under a pretext of seeing what they were about and what their Intentions were relative to their future conduct. in obscure cases there after that transpired with them and the Indians suspicions planted a doubt in the minds of many, that they had made some agreement with the Indians to spare them and property in their incursions

[p. 66[56]]
56
in future inroads that they would make in that Country, that they would on their part make it convenient to give them the items of any thing agitated agains them by the white people. They were very much suspicioned of giveing a full detail of what colonel Callier aimed. The Indians say that they were informed of the movements made by the americans to intercept their ammunition, but they would not say who was their informant ~ as they recieved full light on the american movements and intentions, they thought it best to divide their squadron of men into many gangs by which measure their ammunition would have more chances to reach home. it was one of these partys of men that defeated Col. Calliers Corps of Voluteers, so on their arrival at the hostile camps, they told in a vaunting manner of defeating an immense army of americans and runing them from the field of Battle and as a proof of it displayd. their scalps in their war victory dance. Then and there it was announcd that they would have ample revenge of that part of the state for their unprovoked attack on them, which they too truly verified not long after. They had a particular desire to try their strength with that part of the present state as they would allay a thirst of long standing desire to fight that part

of the country for imposing on them for many years that is their being called too, and obliged to land every time that they passed by Fort Stoddert when it stood on the river Tombigbay which they ever looked on as a grievance, and made them have a spite to that part of the state. The reason why they so resented it on the community is their accounting even an aggression done by an individual a national crime and blaming all people as if they were guilty of the crime, that they unjustly imputed to the soldiers of Fort Stoddert only for their living in the same part of Country that the fort was in ~ On some of the following occurrencies William Weatherford will appear on the stage of action a man who has been celebrated in this predatory war as a leader of the hostile band, but to this period,

[p. 66[57]]

57

he had been shy of them and had, had no concern in their cabals either directly or indirectly but fate so ordered his fortune at that crisis that he was drawn into the war measures of the hostile party in an unpremeditated way, and contrary to his opinion of such foolish undertakings he abhorred their wicked proceedings though he afterwards participated in a conspicuous manner in their war measures as long as he could get followers. nothing could have been farther in his opinion at that time than that he would ever join in their hostile measures. When they first began their fanatical riots of shaveing their heads and painting it red for distinction, makeing encampments and destroying the inoffensive peaceable and well inclined part of the men as witches of a bad class, he could not but feel thoughtfull and to doubt his personal safety should they continue their riotous ways for any length of time, but on a view of their situation in life and overbearing manners he was made to conclude from their actions ingeneral that the storm of their frenzied delusion was in full blast and would blow off like a tornado in a short time, and they would then retract their self deluded errors and become more calm sociable and less devilish toward each other. in order to keep clear of their intrusions or false constructions, that they might make to implicate him in his words or actions, he made it his business to take a trip to Pensacola to get some necessaries for his family consumption. while he was absent down to Pensacola procuring the necessaries for his household comfort, his wifes kinsmen removd. her, tho' he was absent, and all his moveable property to the hostile camps at othlewallee (which was considered as hostile head quarters) above the mouth of line creek. On returning to his home from Pensacola he was as much surprised as perplexed to find his family and property forced into the camps of the ferocious hostile band. it put his mind in dilemma. he knew not what to do to leave his family and property at thier mercy and go down the river to his relatives seemed like parting soul and body. he canvassed the matter in all attitudes and bearings; atlength he concluded on the plan of dissimulation with them. to effect his purpose, he thought it adviseable to hide his disapprobation of the measure they had pursued and patiently await a fit opportunity to

[p. 66[58]]

58

run off with his family and property from under the eyes of the hostile bands. he repaired there likewise expecting to effect his plan of reprisal, but he awaited an opportunity without a chance to effect an escape with his family to the time of the <u>Burnt corn Battle</u> which proved to be too late a date for him to retract with safety on either side ~ Before the <u>burnt corn fight</u> happened, it was known to many of his friends and acquaintances that he had entered the hostile camps, and his reasons for doing so was likewise known to them. all their proceedings in camp was readily told by refugees that run from the nation either Indians or Indian negros. Tho' it was a situation hard on him and his family, and the topic of discourse; and lamented as a hard case by his friends, yet for all that when they were vanquished in battle at Burnt Corn, in the heat of their party rage the vanquished party swore his death on sight, for no other reasons that they could assign for it, than they knew he was at that time in the hostile camps. They likewise knew his reasons for being there. They moreover knew that he had taken no part in their hostilities, or debates for the extension of their depredations on the frontier settlers. He had repeated informations of the threats put out against him, and who made them and that the threats seemed to be made by determined men with a determined intent. This he got from runaway negros who went and joined the hostile Indians to assist in exterminating the white people and be free ~ as the hostile band was determined and ready to commence active operations and depredations on their foe it was necessary for him to be decisive. when he took a view of his situation at that time it was as critical as dangerous. he could see no way to extricate himself with any safety of person and property, for to leave his wife children and effects in the hands of the vigilant hostile band whose watchfulness he could never elude, to make his escape, and to fly alone to those who were his sworn and deathly enemies seemed but the effect of folly and madness, and he could devise no way to explain the reason of his conduct to his former friends, and elude the vigilance of the hostile party so as not to be found out by them and if detected in an attempt to correspond he knew death was his portion and probably of his whole family. They had noticed some appearances of uneasiness, and a coldness in him toward their measures, and they appeared to keep an unusual strict eye on him and his conduct. They had gone so far in their distrust as to accuse him of dissimulation and disaffection to the common cause. it was hard to exculpate himself in the eye of the other party of the circulating report of his joining the hostile party, as he had stayed in the hostile camps so long which he did awaiting an efficient chance to elope with what he had. atlength he ascertained positively that his conduct was implicated irretrievably with both his former friends and acquaintances and he himself proscribed by those that he once considered as unalterable friends. as he was convinced that such was his present standing, he had no choice left to make, but as a dernier alternative to stay with his family tho' against his will and make the best of a bad recourse by taking his fate in the hostile ranks be it bad or worse ~

Before he had given over the Idea of an elopement with his family or determined on the course to pursue, the hostile party held a general council to know what was best for to be done as they were then ready to commence their wishd. for catastrophe that was their extermination of the white people. as a commencement of such a duty, it was concluded to go down the river and make an attack on fort mimbs and fort Pierce. They were about two miles apart. their whole wish and aim was to humble and destroy fort mimbs as they knew that there was a great many men in there that they had devoted to destruction to revenge the burnt corn fight. as they wanted all the advice they could attain on the propriety of such a descent on that place and country, his opinion was asked for the first time, by both the leaders of Bands and by The prophets who descended to ask advise of mortal man. They all asked as with a wish to pay deference to his opinion and views on the practicability of makeing an impression on their hated fort mimbs. as he already knew their determination and that they could not be biassed by him to stop, and divert their views to some other place as an

[p. 66[60]]

60

object worthy of their attention, the die he counted now as cast with him, let what would turn up. on such a reflection he gave them his opinion and views without reserve on the plan that he thought an attack might be made with success. As they then thought that he delivered his sentiments without reserve, thereafter it was perceptible that there was a sudden transition from threats and distrust of his integrity in their cause, to an unbounded confidence and reliance reposed in him in expectation of his better judgment to concert and meet events ~ From the sudden and exalted opinion the hostile band concieved of his talents and understanding they thought he merited distinction, so as the time for active exertions had approached the future operations was entirely left to his guidance and control by all denominations without a competition. The Prophets accordingly submitted themselves to his opinions, and directed others to do so likewise. Paddy Walsh one of their prophets was nominated by the consent of all to the office of head leader of all. Though he acted as head he acted under the imfluence of Weatherfords opinion. The day was set for all the forces to concentrate at the mouth of Flat Creek, and they sent the broken days to all the towns. (The broken days is a bundle of broken parts of twigs about four inches long every piece for one day tied carefully in a bundle. one of the sticks is thrown away at sun rise every day to the last which is the day appointed.). The leaders of different towns on an appointed day collected their warriors of every town separately and held a war dance, and after it was over they started on different routs for the mouth of Flat creek, in the county of monroe, where they were to concentre their whole force and number them, which they did seven hundred and twenty six effective warriors. before they moved from there they held their great war dance. in makeing their descent from there on the Fort they did not move with the despatch which is generally supposed. They were four days going about Fifty miles. in the time they were seen frequently by different persons that were out to see their plantations some as far as twenty five miles from the fort. They generally returned in haste and told where they had

[p. 66[61]]

seen a great many Indians of mounted and a foot that they were on the road that led directly to the fort that their number appeared immense as they could only see one end of them in single file. The informers were generally men of Fort Pierce, so their report was disbelieved, expecting it was told to give them an unnecessary alarm for the diversion of their own fort. in the second instance it could not be supposed by such as was acquainted with Indian mode of warfare, that they would presume to attack a regular fortification knowing it was defended by an hundred and thirty nine men which composed the force of the Fort, from a few Indians and several Indian negros that had run away from Fort Pierce to the nation, which they frequently was doing from that Fort not without it being suspicioned that it was intentionally and covertly done, as their going away never created a word of remark or murmer from the party ~ They informed both Indians and Weatherford of the force of each Fort very near and from them he ascertained who particarly resided in each Fort. The above was his own information and he was likewise informed of the continued hard threats put out against him and by whom they were made; the day before they assauted Fort Mimbs, the whole band of Indians stopped about six miles from the Fort, in the after part of the day to cool and refrest themselves. at that time they saw two mounted men pass on by them, in another road at about three hundred yards distance that led to another ford on the creek that they had just crossed. They were seemingly careless and in a deep conversation. They returned the same way they had gone, in seemingly the same deep conversation, in about the time that it would take to ride to the ford on the creek and Back again. from their manner of riding, they appeared to be under no perceptible alarm, so the Indians were confident from their negligent manner on their return, that they had not been to the ford where the Indians crossed nor seen their trail, when the scout was on their return, many of the Indians urged a pursuit of them to cut them off. But they were not

[p. 66[62]]

allowed to do it, on the inference that the scout had not seen the place that they had crossed at ~ and if they cut them off from the Fort and in the pursuit killed them their not returning to the Fort in time would cause an alarm and search for them, which would cause the India... being seen, and if they escaped from their pursuit it would be the same, and if they were let go on in their entire ignorance of their being there, on their safe return to the Fort they would undoubtedly report there was no enemy to be seen, and the report of the Scout would ensure security and carelessness at the Fort, and a matter of course when they were assaulted they would be unaware of it, and in an unprepared state ~ which proved a fact in that case. The Indian Band not expecting any more Scout on that road went on deliberately after the men, to about three quarters of a mile of the Fort where they halted for the night, to refresh themselves for tomorrows work. after dark and all things was still, Weatherford selected two men that he could confide in and depend on in a case of danger. with them he went to view the plan of and reconnoitre the Fort and the exact situation of it. he pushed his examination of it so far, him and one of his men as to get to the picckets and look through the port holes which was easily done for they were four foot high and about four foot apart all around without ditch or bank. They gained very little insight by their looking through the port holes, as there was but a few glimmering lights scattered about and all looked so obscure and gloomy that he saw very little of the interior situation of the Fort, but by his geting to the fort unpercieved he judged that they were very careless and negligent in guarding the fort, and as they were a moveing about in a careless manner, and conversing on common topics of life, he was sure that the scouts of that Evening had not seen the Indians nor gave any alarm. after trying to see what he could in the Fort, he and his men returned to the army, and by day they were informed of his operations at the Fort that night. The leaders of Bands assisted him in digesting the plan of attact. every man painted red or black and stript to the buff knew

[p. 66[63]]

the part and place he was to act in. as another necessary

measure Paddy Walsh urged as an Omen for them to know by of their being successfull in their assaut, as the old field surrounding the Fort was large that they must run up to the wall without firing a gun, and take possession of the port holes. as the rest were a doing that, that the four men he should select for that purpose he would make invulnerable and proof against a white mans bullet, was to enter the fort and fight inside as long as they thought fit, their safe retreat out of the Fort again, was to be an Omen to them that they were to take the place. accordingly when they ran up to the walls, the four selected men ran in at the gate and raised the war scream and penetrated to the very centre where all got killd. but one, and he quickly retreated out again without a hurt. he was of Jim Boys town, and for his prowess and promptitude in performing that action, on his arrival at home at the war dance, he got the war name of (na ho mah tee o thle ho bo yer which is, the foremost man in danger in time of battle). all their prognostics being arranged and made known and all the men in readiness their army divided into three divesions. They silently moved on to the attack of the Fort on the 30 day of August 1813. Their spies moved a head to see what was acting at the Fort. while they were a trying to take a view of the fort, and their army anxiously a waiting, the Fort drum beat for twelve Oclk. They were sure that they had been seen, and that that was an alarm drum. The word was given to charge. on that the whole body started in full speed for the Fort. though they run up in so large a body they were in less than a hundred yards of the fort gate before they were seen by any one. The gate sentry was engaged looking over the shoulders of a couple playing cards. They run up and raised the war whoop and took possession of three squares of the Fort, and of the ill constructed port holes which was just high enough for their use. There was a cry in the Fort of nothing but, the

Indians the indians. all seemd. in confusion and no one ready, and as they got ready and came out of their houses, they were mostly killed, by the indians that were possessd. of the port holes. The year troops with Major Beasley who commanded all, were killed in a few minutes. There was a dividing wall in the Fort and the year troops had one division of it. What remained of them run into

[p. 66[64]]

the other part that was occupied by the militia and families. Tho' the indians made their assault with steadiness and seeming desperation they were twice repelled by the constancy of the brave whitemen and indians within. The indians at their commencement sit on fire all the houses near the East wall. The fire soon progressd. to the dwelling house that stood in the centre, and so on, so those within were compelled to fight in a case of desperation when they found themselves surrounded by columns of smoke and fire, death dealing bullets, and the unceaseing echo of the war whoop. The indians found themselves so roughly handled in fights once that they drew off for near an hour, and would not have commenced their attack anew, but the negros they had would not cease urgeing them on, untill they saw their mettle was raised, by reciting that they thought it interested them to have the Fort people destroyed. The indians were braved on to the charge, and they renewd. the attack again when they carried the Fort; the people within against all advantages from without, sustained their Fort untill about an hour of sun setting against their assailants, when the heat of the houses that were on fire became so intensely hot in the narrow space they had to occupy, that it was unsupportable with the general want of water that prevailed, for at that time their men was greatly thinned.

besides there was but two houses and a bent behind one, for to shelter them from the enemy, as all the rest were on fire or burnt down, and no attempt could be made of geting water from the well without being killd., as the indians had entire possession of the port holes. as their situation was such as allowed them no chance, and it was their wish to sell their lives at as dear a rate as possible, it was concluded to cut the pickets down at the bent, and go out at it and take their death in a fight in the old field, when the women and children might have a chance to escape, if thought unnecessary or of no avail when they all got out to make their escape who could. the pickets were cut down accordingly where they all went out simultaneously. when once out no one stayed to fight, but every man tried to make his escape to the thicket and swamp ~ on the day priviously to the one the Fort was attacked on, there was a general muster of the men, when there appeared to be seventy six year troops and fifty two effective militia and eleven unfit for duty, makeing one hundred and thirty nine men in all.

[p. 66[65]]

65

of the aforesaid men seventeen made their escape good, when they left one hundred and twenty two killd., and beside them two hundred and one women and children. the whole possee of the Fort of women men and children, at the time that the assault was made numbered three hundred and forty. of that number eleven was taken out alive, as prisoners of war, which leaves the number masscred three hundred and thirteen and twenty Eight, escaped, and taken for prisoner. The hostile Indian loss of what got killed at the fort, by computations made by heads of towns, was thus such as died of their wounds to and after their return to their homes was two hundred and two, and many that got wounded survived. It was reported that their great reduction of men in their ranks, by death, wounds, and other disabities that they got in taking Fort Mimbs; was what caused them not to attempt any thing at that time against Fort Pierce, but many of the Indians as well as white People supposed it was fulfilling some prior understanding, made with some people in ft. Pierce. When the People within the Fort Mimbs began to cut down the Pickets to make their escape out, Weatherford was so near and several others that understood their discourse that from what he heard them say he judged that his mortal enemies were sufficiently humbled. he undoubtedly knew the horrible doom that awaited them, when once they were out of the Fort, or in Indian power. he further knew the Indian mode of war, when they overpowered their enemy in battle by which infuriated rule of theirs, that fate would not discriminate such as he would willingly have saved from death, by intercession from such of them as he was Careless about saving. he so far relented when he thought on their sorrowing and jeopardised situation, that he did not stay to witness the catastrophe pending over their terminated existence. his manly breast that he had unshrinkingly exposed to their, death dealing rifle balls, for during the eventful day, was all at once filled with sorrowing reflections for some he knew to be there, who was once his dearest friends but now separated by unprecedented destiny. his eyes refused to see their mangled end. he turned for his horse abruptly mounted him and rode off for his brothers David Tate's plantation without deigning to look back ~ The night after the conflagration of the fortress and massacre of the

[p. 66[66]]

66

people, and when they had gathered all the horses and all

other property that they could find, they then for the first had time to see into their own situation and reflect on their dear bought atchievement, in takeing the Fort. behold when they stated their positions, they found they were in the error of defect, that of all their men that went into action fully half was killed and disabled and wounded. They could no longer stand the florishing deception of their prophet and commanding leader, for he had before assured them in the positive that when they commenced the assault that he on his part would run round the fort three times, that after he had done that, the force of the Bullets shot from the fort would be dead or fly upwards, none of them could be killed, and they would have nothing to do, but draw their knives and war clubs enter the fort and slay all in it, without fear or danger, as all the men would be in a state of torpitude and paralized. Paddy done as he said he would. he run round the fort the three times, and every time he went round, at the bent where the people got out thereafter he was shot down) however he kept encourageing his men to throw by their fire arms and enter the fort with war club and scalping knife in hand. Those that understood him, that were inside, of the Fort defied them to do it, saying it was what they wished them to try as they were prepared for such a measure. no doubt but the menaces from withing kept them from trying the event. when the bustle of gathering the plunder of the department was over and they had all got together again they once more saw the consequence of their dear bought conquest. They rose in fury at night against the prophet and leading man Paddy Walsh for their loseing so many men by death and wounds. Tho' he was shot through the body himself in three places, it did not excuse him so the Alabamas to get him out of the hands of the infuriated populace took canoes and transported him and themselves up the river to the towassee town as he was of their clan.

The town stood in the bend of the river below the city of Montgomery in Montgomery county ~ They travelled so slow up home by water that they were a length of time getting up to their towns. however their wounded were all Cured in the time as they continually kept reconnoitering the county

[p. 66[67]]

as they passed. up on the west side of the alabama river they found a fort and concluded to take and sack it likewise. The duty of of effecting the enterprise fell on the dog warrior called by the Alabamas Coo le jer which in English is light maker. he took a detachment under his command of between ninety and a hundred men. with them he moved directly to fort sinkfield and made an assault on it. he had no doubt of takeing it easily, from the reports of his reconnoitering parties, but to his surprise and mortification, they had got a reinforcement in the fort, and give him a warm reception, and repulsed him from there with the loss of nine of his men, five killed in the attack and four died of their wounds, afterwards. This attempt on fort sinkfield closed the scenes of their first irruption on the tensaw settlement. The hostile party got a vast number of horses and a great deal of other effects in their pillage of fort Mimbs, and Country from which they concluded that the time had arrived that was spoken of by Tecumseh, and repeatedly confirmed after that by the predictions of their own prophets, that there was to come and be a time, when the Indians would have the lone possession and undisturbed range of all their lands and country, and no white man dare to put his foot thereon without their permission, that such was so decreed, by the great spirit and it must come to pass and so remain ~ After Weatherford mowed down to the attack of

Fort mimbs with Paddy and his adherents Josiah Frances being no warrior did not attend in the expedition with his adherents. he purposely pretended to be very busy erecting a town at that time, on a parcel of ground that he said was pointed out to him, as a spot made sacred by the great spirit, and consecrated lonely for the Indians, and was never to be sullied by the footsteps of the real white man, that there was a destructive barrier circled all round it, which a white man could not pass over alive. in order to increase the population of it, and as a way to invite permanent settlers of all such as had quit the camps at othle wal lee which was almost turned to a Babel to them, when they had a disperson, for there had been an inviollable confusion of Languages during their stay together, he by inspiration announced that his place was and had been named afore Ecun-a cha ga which in English is sacred or beloved ground.

[p. 66[68]]
68

When the lower town hostile Indians had wreeked their vengeance on the tensaw setlers by a general massacree of them and their families on their return home they had to go to their respective towns as the othle_wal le residents through their Idleness; and waste of their subsistance had brought themselves to hunger and a general dispersion to their former homes again.

after their victorious expedition and return home the hostile Indians Vaunted mightily of their deed and made a great display and exposition of their plundered wealth to them that had staid at home in ease and Idleness. they were mostly of Francis's adherents who could not but see Their own poverty; and the sudden wealth of the opposite party. They on reflection began to say that they would have participated of such affluence had they not followed the idle advice of Francis to stay at home and build the sacred town. They very rightly imputed his stay and care of buildings to nothing but a pretext to hide his fear and cowardice; as he was in a fair way of becomeing as contemptable among his adherents As the other partys ~ as he knew from the recent massacre of the tenants of Ft. Mimbs that there could be no formidable enemy left to annoy him and his men and with all this he understanteng from negro prisoners that there ware many Horses in the Tensaw river fields that could be got by going for, he told the men of his party that from his foreknowledge he could tell them in the positive that if they would follow him to the same country that they would get nearly as much booty and property as the other party. Accordingly there followed him to the gleaning upwards of one hundred and Eighty war men who gathered all the horses that were overlooked and left by the others and burned all the dwelling houses saw mills &c. They dug up got and destroyed an immense quantity of house hold furniture being shewn by the negro prisoners where such had been buried by their former owners on their going to the unfortunate fortress ~

[p. 66[69]]

69

he effected his expedition and never encountered an enemy and returned as he thought covered with laurels of glory. by his makeing the expedition he so far gained his ascendancy over the community of his original townsmen as to get them into his holy town. many that lived in the vicinity were induced from the following reasons to go into the town viz. hearing that the white people were on the alert a raising and embodying troops on the tombigbay side from the west which armament they knew must be for the purpose of chastising them and town for their horrid deeds and depredations. as it was the lowest down and next to the White Settlements it was the receptakle of every runaway negro who all confirmed the story of the american armament but they carelessly carried on their town building without seeming to mind such reports to near the Christmas When they were informed by one of their swift look out men that he had seen near the town of Claiborne a very large army of Whitemen moveing up the river on the big road which report was every day confirmed by their runners for four days on which day they were attacked by Genl. Claiborne. They returned the Genls. salute for one round and began to give way and cross the river with their prophet at their head to seek safety on that side. as the whitepeople they saw had crossd. Francis' enchanted death-dealing barrier round their town, his adherents were very much shaken in their hitherto firm reliance in the foresight of their prophet and leader and fled after him cheerfully from the place where they had awaited to meet the attack of the enemy in the woods bordering the holy ground town to see their white pursuers pass the enchanted line likewise without droping dead. They then undeniably percieved that their purifications and his incantations of night before was not strong anough to save them and the holy ground town from destruction. The prophet led the way and shewed them how to escape danger by flight and swiming and not fight for his holy made ground and and dwelling ~

[p. 66[70]]
70

Though the prophet and his party who lived on the holy ground left the field of battle and made their escape the contention did not cease with their runing off with the loss of a few warriors, for William Weatherford kept it up a while longer. he happened there by chance on this wise. When he and McPherson a half breed of scotch and Indian, heard from their swift and distant runners a few days before they were attacked, that he had seen an army of white men both horse and foot a comeing up the big road, they and their friends as they were a living on the big road, concluded as it was not Safe to stay there, that they would go down the big swamp creek and to the holy ground town, by which removal they would be off of the big road, and be in more force in the town when invaded as they were sure and conscious that an attack was intended by the aforesaid army; as they purposed to reinforce Francis and his followers by their removal to his town. Weatherford went with three more and took a deliberate view of the approaching army about two miles from the town. he knew that the Indians were in no way able to withstand such a force and equipments. he returnd. and made preparations to repel them if possible with a force of about two hundred men or a little more. when the war men of town heard of their near approach and went in array to meet them Weatherford, McPherson and their neighbors about thirty men joined and went with them. They and the runaway negros were all determined men. They meant to give the foe as good a fight as possible, after the defection and total desertion of Francis and his followers. Then it was that the reinforcement and runaway negros had to sustain the battle in a retreating fight. while they were earnestly fighting to check them untill the town women and children could hide some of their stuff and make their escape good a runner came to them and gave them the new that they about being surrounded by a squdron of horsemen and foot who were a trying to close their lines on the rear of the town. They all quickly retreated Some to save themselves and others their horses and to make a trial of effecting an escape at an open space of ground where the two were not closed. The Indians and negros being mostly afoot saved themselves by swiming over the river. John Moniac and two others went through before the lines were closed.

[p. 66[71]]

71

Weatherford and McPherson when mounted took a view of the lines to see if there was any gap that would admit of their escape, found all closed and makeing a move for the centre to fight them they were unable, and as to surrendering and being prisoners to an army from that quarter they would prefer death in any way or form. The only avenue that occured to them whereat to make an escape left for them was to leap off of a bluff at the junction of the creek and river between fifty and sixty feet high which itself was death or liberty. Weatherford being mounted on the swift and mettlesome Courser Called the Abboninair who in part belonged to Benjamin Baldwin Esqr. of Macon County, he knew his mettle and and docile disposition to the will of his rider and that he would not fly aside from any direction given him more especially if urged by the spur he proposed takeing the first leap from off of the bluff. he rode his horse up to the margin and let him see it then reined him about nearly thirty yards, took his rifle in hand and struck of in a canter for the bluff and touched him With the Spur, when the generous beast leapt off as tho he meant to reach the other or opposite Shore. he said he seemd. to go right straight forward for upwards of thirty feet. then he turned nearly head down and kept a curving flight till he struck the water. he and his horse separated long before he struck the water. Then they swam a shore together gun and all unhurt. When he made the shore he saw his flight repeated by McPherson when he took his flight. he said the sight was awfully curious for to see a man and horse fly through the air like a cormorant or fish Eagle when he pounces on a fish. as they all got to Shore unhurt from their jump, they cleared themselves. Their friends who swam the river went up and recrossd. bearing the news of the destruction of the holy ground town, wherever they went ~ in their conflict with Genl. Claiborne they supposed that they lost in killed about thirty men to say about 20 Warriors and 7 run a way negros who joined the Indians with the expectation of being free, when they and the Indians should conquer and destroy the white people according to the say of the prophets. in a few days after the fight Francis and his men returnd. to see about their dead, and get their household stuff they had buried there. instead of their houses they found only the smoke and ashes ~

[p. 66[72]]
72

The burning of the Ocanachaga gave relief to the white people of the settlements down the river. it finally closed the hostile operations and incursions of magnatude of the lower towns Indians, or more appropos the parties of Francis and Paddy. The latter moved to the Othlewalle's camps again where they were necessarily to embody their force as they expected an immediate attack from Georgia or Mississippi or perhaps from both places at once ~ as I have taken an historical view of Francis from his first turning to a prophet to this period I shall here close the events of his after life, as I had contemplated to do when I announced the destruction of the holy ground in detail before the Autussee battle which tranpired a month or more before that of the holy ground. Josiah Francis whose father was a residentor of Cosawda for many years it is said was a black smith of French parents. They were both very superstious (that is Josiahs parents) and his parents raised him as an Indian and in Indian superstitious Ideas, so it was not a great change in him to admire Tecumsehs pretance of knowing future events, but he was of a timid nature so the burning of the holy ground town, so alarmed him that he had no time to think of prophecying in serious terms of mischief, but in his terror and incertitude of events, his thoughts were engrossd. to know how he and his few adherents were to make a timely and safe escape to Pensacola for security out of a storm that he could see without revelation portending an overturn of the nation and its customs. he and his party moved to Pensacola atlength where he imfluenced the Indians to join Major Nicoll who then commanded the british force on this station. he attended capt. woodbine in their attack of Mobille point. then he returned to Pensacola and staid there untill after the failure of the british at New Orleans, when he was carried to England by Major. Nicoll with the promise of his being well recieved by the King or his ministers for his indefatigable Exertions to imfluence the hostile tribes in favour of England. on his departure for europe he directed his family, to await his return in the seminoles. he was accompanied by a Cosawda chief called Moulton. They returned with Messas. Ambrister and Arbuthnot. They soon began to give the Seminoles friendly english talks. at length by a mistake they went on board of an American Gun Boat where they were arrested, and by an order of Genl. Jackson they closed their eventful life by being hung on the yard arms of the Gun boat ~

[p. 66[73]]

73

Francis was a man of no talent very still and

reserved in his manners in the ordinary scenes of life he was of no turn to command respect or esteem but it need not be doubted but he by his fanatical pretensions to call a future knowledge of things overbalanced all sober reason in his tribe which led to their wild and thoughtless outbreaking, so he became one of a few that caused the downfall of the Ispocaga tribes.

I must in this place apologise to the reader for my digressing from the ordinary maxims of history by narrate-ing the fall of the holy ground town before the battle of the Autussees which latter was upwards of a month previous, but I done it in the first instane as I was treating of Francis's tranactions not to disconnect it till I hung him up in a state of inaction which I have effected, so I shall revert back nearly two months to relate the transactions of their body politic, from the time that Genl. Jackson entered the nation and destroyd the littappuche and Tallashatche and dis-comfitted the largest armament that they ever embodied. The hostiles had began to be more cautious and think of manner and means by which they might evade a total annihilation of their nation, and by paying more attention to their scattered state of dwellings, and removing them so as to make their situations more dense that they could then attend better to their local concerns of war. They had not only seen but felt the impropriety of their conduct in haveing a war at the door of every town, and the repeling of the foe to be left to be done alone by the warriors of each town and village that should chance to be attacked, that the weakness of even their largest towns would be inevitably overthrown when brought into single contact with an embodied and well equipt army of white people, that their small towns in their present local situations must fall one by one and be an easy prey to the invader, untill the nation by such a piecemeal would be consumed, so the conclusion in the debating council of their prophets and head warriors of towns was, that certain named towns, should be selected and embraced in such demarkations pointed out, about to form and assimilate different bodies over all the nation at particular places of natural strength and by Such means those different stations or encampments would each

[p. 66[73a]]
73a
separately be strong anough to contend with and repel any invading army that might attack them. according to the aforesaid conclusion

[p. 66[74]]

74

they pitched on the Othlewalle (or Cluwallee) and the Autussee as places of Convenience in which places they were in the habit of frequenting embodying at and dispersing in part for the want of provisions as they had at their outsetting of hostillities wantonly destroyd. nearly all that they could get at. So these two stations made on the Tallapoosy were for all townsmen from the Tallassee to Welumka and as low down the river as the bend below the City of Montgomery to resort to for safety in case of an incursion of the Enemy. The Autussee Station was the most respectable in men numbering Over and Under a Thousand Warriors and The Othlewallee Upwards at all times of five Hundred men. both Stations looked on Paddy as their prophetic commander tho he principally resided at the Cluwallee Camps. both Camps had been on the alarm and look out e'en before the fall of the two autussee towns and had kept their swift runners on the look out towards the Talladega and hillabees for they had no idea of any other enemy being out than the Tennesseeans which army they expected to have the fighting of for near a month back as they had an idea of their expeditions movements and prompt fighting. They could likewise get the news con-tially from run a way negro's that great preparation was makeing of men and provisions in Mississippi and Georgia for an irruption but that such invasion would not transpire untill towards the Spring of the ensuing year. They had not heard for some time for Certain of the movements of the Tennessee troops only that they were in the nation. Their view of all circumstances put together, was that the fient of inaction that pervaded the times was in order to lull them into inattention and inaction. When the white people percieved this, that they intended to press on them all at once and crush them with an Overwhelming force according to plans now concerting in this time of seeming inaction and that the Tennessee troops would and were quiet only untill they got a recruit of men or supply of provisions to commence, that the first movement would be a signal for a general invasion. if it was so as they contemplated they were determined to meet the foe at all hazards and take death if so ordained for a man could die but once, so when the two Autussee towns was attacked by Genl. Floyd

[p. 66[75]]

the Cluwallees were confident of an immediate brush themselves with the Georgians or Tennesseeans. They said they had been and were still in hourly expectancy of such an event, so after they had held their meeting and it was ascertained and that all things yet remained quiet and still, Coosa micco the commander and head of the Autussee town sent for his confidential and intimate friend a Cluwallee Called Te wa sub buk le. he was one of the principal prophets and Chief in Command of his townsmen. he wanted to consult him on the propriety of defensive or Operative measures which of the two had best be pursued in future. They had been and were still in deep and private convesaton about three or fours hour before day, when a man who had Camped out that night for an early Turky hunt came runing into town and announced the near approach of a large army of white people. as they had long expected it they were not dismayed or surprised. there was an instant order for the infirm Old men to cross the river with the women Children and negros and disperse them into places of safety down below the Othlewallee camp and if they succeeded in repeling the foe of which they had no doubt the foe being dispersed, they would receive word to return. the aforesd. matters and dispositions being hastily arranged Te wa sub buk ly then proposed for Coosa micco to still keep the command of the upper Autusse Town near the mouth of the Callebee creek, where the Tallasees under the McQueans and the Autussees were stationed and that he must receive the onset of the enemy in the front edge of the town, and he would go down to the other part of the town which stood near a half mile below which was composed of Warriors from different minor towns out of the fork between the two rivers. The movements of that body he intended to direct himself, and await the enemys onset in the border of the town. They had scarcely time to make known to each other the hasty plans of disposing their men to meet the Onset of the enemy when their runner announced to them that the enemy had made his appearance in the bordering woods of the town, and that he was a makeing movements which the runner supposed to be preparing for an attack on the town. Then they parted each of 'em to his command to meet no more, confident of an attack of the white men. The variously expecting Indians

[p. 66[76]]

Awaited it untill day light, when expectation Ceased in reality for Coosa micco rather glader than otherwise saw the army of White people moveing forward and commence their attack with small arms and cannon. he called his men to arrange themselves properly and meet the enemy. he returned their salute and accompanied it with general war whoop. he encouraged his men to fight brave and calmly without shrinking back and not to fearfully waste their fire. he tried to infuse his spirit of fighting into them both by words and action. while he was encourageing and exorting his men all he could to the fight and for them to do it without fear and exert themselves, the news was brought to him and the McQueans that Te-wa-sub-buk-le the prophet was killed, and that the warriors appeared all in the notion to disperse, and were a giving ground very rapidly. On hearing this he mounted his horse and made speed for the lower town warriors to try if he could repair damages, but the case was scarce retrievable for the greater part of 'em was on the retreat makeing for the ponds of water just against their habitations. they were in a panic, after they had been charged by the horsemen. he rallied and stopped some of them. with them he thought to turn the left flank of the american troop and get in their rear which he concieved if he could do it would cause them to rally and encourage them to stay and fight for he saw that they were not willing to fight front to front. in his trying to turn their flank he said, that let him turn as far or what way he would, that the enemy would always present a solid front untill they began to mix together in mortal strife. by the time he reached the (thlaw a nub ba) that is the (uppermost level) he began to see his own town men in the chace of defalt. they had irretrievably gave ground for to ensconce themselves in the big reed brake which convinced him without words that he was whipt and overcome, as he was himself badly wounded in two places with bullets and chopped across the cheek by a sword and his horse shot through the neck and body his warriors in a panic takeing the great reed brake to hide in of near a quarter of a mile wide laying on the S. E. part of the town and he being very faint with the loss of blood, he dismounted atlength himself and took into the reed brake and gave up the Autussee town and battle to the Conquerors ~ before the commencement of the battle

[p. 66[77]]
77
Coosa Micco and Te-wa-sub-buk-le had sent a very pressing word to the Cluwallee Camps, that they were about being atteked and to come to their assistance; but they never Came nor so much as started. Why Paddy never came to their assistance I could never ascertain. In said Autussee battle the hostiles supposed that they lost in killed probably Eighty men and upwards of a hundred wounded ~ Their compete defeat with the burning of their town broke up the hostile settlement in the Autussees. it gave them a complete scare and set them to rambleing. many of them took up their quarters in the Othlewallee camps. some made their way with their families to inaccessible places in the swamps of the forest and others went for pensacola for safety among the Spaniards. The hostile camps by this time began to feel the want of ammunition there being a general scarcity of that article among them, so there was a general meeting called by the hostile chiefs and prophets, to take into view their situation and state of affairs. among the rest they wanted to see and sent for W. Weatherford to attend. he had secluded and confined himself to his home ever since the affair of the Talladega fort. when he recieved

their request he attended at the Cluwallee camp. accordingly when the subject was Opened by the prophets, Paddy and High-Headed Jim they mentioned the alarming state of their affairs situated as they were through the scarcity and general want of powder and lead in every department, that on a strict examination they had made for the articles among the warriors it was a notorious fact that they could not stand another battle as at the Autussees for the want of powder and lead and as Weatherford had assisted High-Headed Jim who the Indians called Cussetaw Haujo on a former occasion of the like nature in the commencement of their hostilities and had succeeded in geting a supply of the two articles from the authorities of of spain, therefore that they all had deemed them as the men best qulified to go to Pensacola with a sufficient escort to ensure them safely back with the powder and lead they might get, so it was agreed to according to the wish of the prophetic authorities high head being one of the prophets himself. The day being appointed to start they took an escort of Three hundd. and ninety mounted men and pursued their way to Pensacola to see their good friend the Spanish Governor.

[p. 66[78]]

78

On their arrival in that metropolis in pursuance of the mission from the hostile authorities they demanded to have an audience and a Tete a tete with his Excellency. in their Tete a tete they pleased his Excellency so well that he made them a present of three horse loads of powder and lead with which they returned to the Cluwallee camps and on their safe return once more revived the drooping Spirits of that section of the hostile party. They were high in spirit, and revived their neglected war dances all through their haveing once more a plenty of powder and lead, but in the midst of their joy and festivities, and their envoys had scarcely got rested from their long and troublesome missionary journey, when it was announced to them by one of their swift runners that he had seen a large army of Georgians on their march with cannon in their train comeing along the Georgia road. on this news Paddy immediately sent swift runners to all persons, places of encampments and towns for the warriors to rendezvous at the Othlewallee camps. the warriors all attended to the words promptly and with dispatch. when they had all assembled they were informed by the prophet, that the white men had and were a forming a Camp on the level of (Chufukna wockna) which is the spike horn bucks bed) and it was their business and interest to fight dislodge them before they made their camp too strong. The whole force marhed up to the west side of Callebee in the evening about a mile from the american Camp. There they numbered their men twelve hundred and seventy four warriors Stript and painted red, and all in readiness to give the camp of the enemy a night encounter. Then the question was proposed by the chiefs and leaders of twownsmen, in what manner and way was the action to commence and be conducted. The plan of onset was left by the chiefs and and prophets of the hostile band, to be regulated by four men viz. the leading prophet Paddy Walsh, McGilliveray, Weatherford and high head Jim. Paddy gave his Opinion first for all the men to be ready and near at hand to the american camp and to make their attack on them as they were about going to sleep and their onset to be against two squares of the camp, and let the attack when made be close and severe and if they made any impression to advantage against the enemys camp by or before day light to keep up the fight to the effect for or against them, and if by dawn of day they made no perceptible impression on the enemy, he would say break of in a retreat and quit the fight. Paddys plan was sanctioned only by High-Head-Jim. McGilliveray and Weatherford dissented from Paddys plan, saying that it seemed to them that Paddys proposd. manner for the fight was only to encounter the enemy saying I am to be defeated in the end as man could not fight hards with a limit on himself in a time to run off, that for their parts when they fought that they fought as long as they could get or see any chance that they wanted no limitations in their battle and then to run off. Weatherford then said that he would propose his idea of a plan. he proposed to begin at the same time of night, as the white peoples fashion of camping was, for all the commanding officers to take their place in the centre of the square of Camps his invariable opinion was that Paddy had better take three hundred men or more if he thought fit. let them take rifle and Tomahawk in hand and move up slily to one of the squares raise the scream and make an opening through it with the tomahawk, at the same time the rest of their red painted men to make a Charging attack on two other squares while this was operating, and in the confusion that must ensue the three hundd. men in the hollow square must endeavor to Tomahawk and kill all the officers and fight their way out at the same square where they went in, and as it was the manner of the white people to fight only in the manner and way that they were directed by their officers that a great confusion must ensue in their army without any to give necessary Orders on the loss of their officers, that such a confusion would give the assailants of the two squares a chance unquestionably of destructively penetrating their two squares into the camps at the same time the three hundred men when out of the Alignment would keep the line they first penetrated in hasty business. eventually the common soldiers not knowing what to do must squander from their encampment for the woods and homeward. The two prophets recriminated on Weatherford in a very authorative and prophetic manner, and seemed to shudder at some hidden motive in it as they would at a contagious pestilence. at length they said that it was a measure of insanity and desperation, that it was a sure and unnessary sacrifise of three hundred men, and Paddy

[p. 66[80]]
80
said that it seemed to him by Weatherfords plan of attack and sactioned by McGilliveray that they wished to distinguish him and jeopardise his life in trying publicly to enfore his commanding and attempting to atchieve a measure he was sure of destruction to him and many others, an undertaking that neither of them dare not undertake themselves. on this insinuation and public arraignment of their prowess and courage the two Weatherford and McGilliveray jumped up upon their feet and said retorting on Paddy for his compliment that they dared to do what was proposed for him to do as a compliment and they were willing one or both to lead that number of painted men to where it was said for them to be led and perform said action or die in the attempt that they did not put so great a value on their life nor regard the loss of it in so precious a light as Paddy appeared to be about the risque of his. They said that they were daily convincd. that a man was born to die, and that he could but loss his life once. They remarked they would prefer death to a fearful neglect of duty to their country and its liberties. Then there was a call made for that number of

red painted men, but a very few offered their attendance for the onset on one of the lines of the american camp, because their debate and Collision was publicly made, and they all knew the prophet had spoken against the measure and plan of attack as if by inspiration. Weatherford took their neglect of his advice and offers of service as a public insult. after their nominating him for one of four to adjust a plan of attack on the enemy his high ideas of honor did not admit him to fight on Paddys plan after publicly inveighing of it so he told Paddy that it was his intention to go home again and let him fight his cautious half fights if he was determin'd. so to do and welcome; so after that he and friends that came with him mounted their horses and made for home that same night. Paddy Walsh being left to follow the dictates of his own mind, conducted his men across the Callebee Creek and assaulted the georgia army according to his proposed plan, of attack, and in the morning after the nights encounter was severely raced with loss. in the battle he lost in killd. about 406 warriors, as to his wounded they could not guess the number.

[p. 66[81]]

81

They lost but one man of importance and consequence to them in their attack. it was high head Jim or Cussetaw Haujo. he was one of their greatest warriors and principal Prophets. William McGilliveray though highly insulted by the prophets that evening in their debate never theless he laid all irritation of mind aside and accompanied Paddy in order to be with and bear his part with his townsmen in the approaching battle of that night. he participated in the defeat and hard race for an escape in the morning from the battle ground. Paddy made his escape that fatal morning tho he was very badly wounded ~ Their defeat at

Callebee was fatal to them. it closed the hostile operations of the lower Towns and finally broke up their hostile unity and embodying at any place for hostile purposes ever after that. it silenced the old and new war dance and whoop of many of their most conspicuous warriors for odious practices at their first outbreaking for the ruthless war. none of the lower towns chiefs ever entered the battle field after the callabee affair, but appeared to be paralised and inattentive to national affairs. They mostly spent their time carelessly inactive, without it was a few indigent ones who were innately prone to mischief. They occasionally made predatory excursions down the river into the settlements of white people, where they were many times so far interested as to kill the owner in order to get his plunder and horse, and in a few instances they killed up whole families and plundered the house and burnt it. Their marauding parties confined themselves in their excursions principally to Monroe and Clark counties. The lower towns appeared to have a spite at the people of that department more than any other, and kept up their hostilities untill the horse shoe bend was taken and the last of their forces destroyed by Genl. Jackson. when the hosile party heard that menawway or in common called Kelisennehaw had laid by his strong objections to his towns painting for the war and that he had at length agreed to their painting and painted himself likewise, they were very much elated at the news, always having had an exalted opinion of his skill and prowess in Indian warfare, but when they heard that after his many conflicts with the Tennessee army that he was destoyd. with his fortification at the horse shoe they then sunk in their opinion of themselves. They began to believe in the instabilities of fortune and transitory scenes of war, ever after they heard of Menawways destruction. The whole possee of them, appeared desirous to get out of the reach of harm and if possible to live neutral on neutral grounds. Their retributive spirit for retaliation and war was broke and cool. There was no consistancy in any thing they projected or done. Their incertitude brought on a dejection of mind and made them seek a shelter in some other place and quit their home and nation where they were fearful hourly of having to encounter a powerful and fortunate enemy, a foe that they had often tried and could not withstand. The Ispocaga or creek tribe, as they could not in their national home find that ease of mind, but were in a torture through the anxieties always prevalent in the days of misfortune made their way for Pensacola in Spanish Florida to get a shelter and a little respite from their apprehensions of dire distruction ~ I think as I made a short Biography of the latter end of the prophet Francis, that it would not be taken a miss in me by the reader to try an exposition of the most prominent tranactions of Paddys latter days to the gallows whilst I am treating of the lower Towns & and their exit. James Walsh the father of Paddy was a south carolinaan who in the American revolution was a despisable Murdering Swamp Tory which caused him after the close of that contest to leave that country where he had perpetrated so many bad crimes and settle himself in the creek nation, where he became the father of Paddy who lost his father while he was very young so of course he was raised as other alabama Indians are in a State of nature without knowing the restraints of mind. Paddy was a man under the ordinary size of men, of a stature not exceeding five foot two or three

Inches in height. the hair of his head came very low on his forehed and a noted wide mouth which made him look most inhumanly ugly. he was a great Indian linguist speaking the creek alabama chickasaw & Choctaw languages fluently. he was a great natural orator both persuasive and commanding. he was so deep in his manner of reasoning, and gifted with such an easy flow of Eloquence that no indian would or could withstand him on any point that he pretended to uphold. he was a noted brave man and never was known to Shrink from a daring action but once and that was when he refused to enter Genl. Floyds lines at the Callebee battle for which refusal he

[p. 66[83]]

83

pretended to have his reasons. after he was defeated and wounded at Callebee he told his alabama people that he was conscious that the Indians were unable to fight the white people with any success in battle array, wherefore it was his studied opinion that they had better go to Pensacola and be out of the way of harm till the nation could effect a peace which bad circumstances would oblige them to do if they could. as for his own part as he was wounded and that it would take sometime doctoring to cure him during which time he had thought it for the best, to go down the river with his relations in their canoes, and go up Some cane brake creek where they could not be found nor their canoes untill he got well. after he got well, as it had become a natural principle in him to hate the white people, it was his wish to be in feud with them so long as he lived. he never would miss a chance of destroying one of ‘em when it occured, so he and his relations ensconced themselves. after he got well in the cane brakes he moved successively down the river, as low down as a place called the standing peach tree, where he got stationed for near a year. One day when he and five or six of his men were a sauntering on a sand shoal, they saw a boat comeing down the river with seven men on board apparent from their caps to be of the army. The Indians went upon the bank of the river for fear of being seen by them.. When the boat got near sand Bank they turned her and landed on the upperside of the sand bank. after they had got out they made for some shade trees near where the Indians were hid with somewhat to eat. just as they were commenceing to eat the Indians fired on them and killed three of them. The survivors made for their boat. The Indians made for there likewise to cut them off from their guns but the soldiers got to her first and got their muskets and fired on them and wounded three of them. then the officer orderd. a charge of the bayonet when the run the Indians off of the sand bank and returned to Get their boat off. in the mean time the Indians had loaded their guns and charged on them. in their charge the soldiers killed one of 'em. Then the Indians deliberately killed all but the officer and one man who drifted against the bank. The officer picked up a Musket and shot one of them down, when his brother killed ... officer and they took the survivor a prisoner and kept him with them near two months before he cut his own throat. The officer was named Wilcox.

[p. 66[84]]
84
Their prisoner told them that he was a lieutenant of the army sent on business with command of the men to Fort Claiborne and that his regiment lay at Fort Jackson. after this transaction Paddy moved to the west side of the river and lay in them cane brakes conceald for some time, before he attempted any thing, which when he done it he said it was to retaliate on the white people for what they had done

to his people. it got norated that the Indians were in large numbers about the lower standing peach tree, upon which noration a party embodied in clark county and went to kell them up and run them from there. in their expedition they went to the camp of and killd. Paddy aunt. for to retaliate for the murder of his aunt he killd. two men Joseph Foster and Joseph Milstead and broke up the new settlement after which Genl. Gaines sent a Lieut. Nelson and a command of men who got holt of the dog warrior who betrayd. Paddy into his hands. he carried him to Fort Claiborne with another youngster to be kept by the military untill he could be tried for his notorious deeds. in about six weeks they made their escape from the guard. the Indians fearing the consequences of his escape from custody give him up again and at claiborne he was tried for the murders he had committed and convicted of the crimes without any evidence for or against him only the say of a liing interpreter who give a false answers to the court saying that he acknowledged the deed and give himself great credit for it saying that it was no more than he intended doing again. on the interpretation he was found guilty and hung at the Fort Claiborne. Tho' he was small ugly and a diminutive man in his personal appearance he was the greatest prophetic warrior that the Ispocaga or creek tribe ever had. after the hostile band was got into active series of war he was their leader to war and battle. if he had been more pacific in his disposition toward the U. S he could from the run of imfluence he had at different times he could have turned the Scale of war to peace a saved the great effusion of blood that he was the cause of through his wicked prophecies. now as I have carried the lower towns to their ... dissertion of their nation I shall fall back two or three months and revive the history of the Upper towns of the coosa and Tallapoosa in their different attitudes and collision in war.

[p. 67]

Mt. Pleasant Ala Feb 21st 1874

Mr. L C Draper Corr Secy

Dear Sir

Yours of the 13th ult came to hand yesterday. I was pleased to learn that the papers reached you safely, & that you deem the narative worth publishing.

As I have before stated, I refered you to Dr. Maiben for facts relating to my Father. I also wrote to him to that effect. I inclose his reply to me.

I do not remember the precise time I received your letter & 5 books, but I replied immediately, acknowledging their receipt. I informed you that parcels numbered 3, 4, 5, 6, & 7 reached us & that 2 were missing but did not expect you to replace them as you are under no obligations to do so.

I have a borrowed copy of Gen T. S. Woodward's letters, will try to get it for you, if I fail I will try to get one in Mobile, & forward it to you.

[p. 67[1]]

You ask me to send you the exact date of my fathers death. If I am not mistaken I wrote father died on the 25th of November. Subsequently, I have been to Mothers & was looking over to records & found that he died of the 22nd of November 1845. Please correct this mistake. We have no date of his birth.

A short time prior to my removal to this place in 1849, I looked over all his papers. Such as I thought would ever be of any use I brought with me, the remainder I left with a sister of mine. She & her husband have both been dead several years. So the diary is lost.

The littler I know relative to Billy Weatherfords career I will write down & forward it to you. I shall write soon, & give the addresses of his 2 sons.

Mr. Driesbachs address
James D. Driesbach
Mt Pleasant
Baldwin County Ala

Perhaps it is necessary to state that Dr. Maiben is a popular Physician, & most respectible, & highly influential Citizen of this State & county.

Your friend
Jos N. Stiggins

[p. 68]

Jan 26th 1874.

Mr J N Stiggins
Dear Sir

In reply to yours of the 8th only received yesterday I beg to state that I find him your father George Stiggins ... some 58 years ago he was the ... middle age and a mutual Attraction grew up between us from the fact of our both enjoying a keen sense of the ludicrous. The extent of my professional ... would have ... was so tired out that I felt relief at sight of your father and in listening to his apparently exhaustless fund of anecdotes.

[p. 68[1]]
pair of ...ely and expressive black eyes a ... good ...meral face and a ... intense fine ... eloquent and facile ... narrative ... at the period your father and myself for at that he was still ... Genl. ... and his annals with Indians and ... your father was contemporary and such an ... of necessity had ... which he detailed with most Entertaining and really interesting ... your father ... to the Creek Nation. I parted with him with regret, and though I met him Afterwards

[p. 68[2]]
it was but for a short period. If anything written about or ... it can be made ... of George Stiggins... will be well repaid for Any little trouble it may have given.

... was written by my daughter. My failing ... imperfections ...ing. It is my ... that Any manuscript of his must prove interesting.

Respectfully ...
R. Maiben

[p. 69]

28th Feb 1874

L. C. Draper Esq
Dear Sir

Yours of the 15th and the book so kindly forwarded have been received.

My first knowledge of Goe Stiggins was some fifty years ago. He was then a comely, portly, man of middle age, both of us gifted with a keen sense of the ludicrous soon led to consideable intimacy. Stiggins abounded in anecdote of the most varied character and possesing a juicy mouth great fluency of speech and geniality of Manner he gave an interest to any thing he uttered in a way Seldom Arrived at by the Most Studied orator. he was entirely Simple & unpretending and our region of country comparatively new as a State though possesing White Settlers for Many years as a Territory gave a novelty to his Anecdotes intensely interesting to one like myself at the time entirely unaccustomed to that State of Society. Many a hard days riding with occasional Serious considerations were Chased and Alleviated by Meeting Stiggins on the way Side but unfortunately that very easy, cheerful, thoughlessness induced in myself a forgetfulness of any thing but the passing pleasure of the moment. Gen. Jackson and his encampment, The Massacre at Mims and the warrior Weatherford & his recent death were all

[p. 69[1]]

Subjects of his Conversation but unfortunately of only passing interest entirely unrecorded until now. Seventy five years are exerting their benumbing influence on body and intellect. The fact is My dear Sir nothing short of your gentlemanly urgency would have induced me to write as I have done and you must extend a charitable consideration to any failure to give you the information you wished for.

If there be any connection with the Newberry Mabins I know it not originally Scots and Irish from the days of Cromwell. I was Myself born in Newark N. J. you must regard this as Self inflicted.

Respectfully
R Maiben

[p. 70]

South Carolina.
Richard Winn, Indian Supt.
Yazoo Settlement.

PURSUANT TO
An Ordinance of Congress
Of the 7th of August, 1786,
I give this Public Notice,

THAT none but citizens of the United States will be permitted in future to reside among or trade with any Indian nation whatever, southward of the River Ohio, which citizen or citizens, under the penalty of Five Hundred Dollars in case of failure, must previously obtain a licence from me for that purpose, producing at the time a certificate from the executive of any state, under the seal of such state, of their character and qualification: --- each licence, on paying Fifty Dollars, to continue in force one year, and such person or persons must also give bond and surety to me in the sum of Three Thousand Dollars, for his or their strict adherence to and observance of such rules and regulations as Congress may from time to time establish for the government of the Indian trade, &c. Permits or passports for travelling through the Indian territories, will be granted to none but citizens of the United-States, whose business must be made known on application to me.

As the above is consonant to the resolves of Congress, and as sufficient power is vested in me to restrain, by force, such as may wilfully neglect the notice here given, I expect every due attention will be paid to this by those whom it may concern.

RICHARD WINN,
SUPERINTENDANT.

Charleston: Printed by Markland & McIver, No. 47, Bay.

[p. 71[1]]

father ... continuing with ... motion, therefore let me a... the most timely manner what you do ... such time as I hear from Congress as ... supplies to facilitate the ... I shall ... the ... to be ... both ...

Richard ...
...

[p. 71[2]]

Richd. Winn
Aug. 29th 1788
ad... to ... Martin
Co ⓢ S... Tipt. Hubbard
To direct his ... against ...

[p. 72]

Cha... Ton
So. Carolina
March 7th 1790

Sir

Yours by Mr. Metzgar of the 15th of February last from Washington District North Carolina came to hand some few Days past. This will be communicated to You through the means of James O'Fallon Esqre. one of the late Captains of the fourth Georgia Battalion & late one of the Senior Physicians of the Hospital of the United States.

It is with pleasure I can inform every welwisher to our Yazoo Settlement that our Business is perfectly Sanctioned by a Legislative Act of Georgia. I passed into a Grant we hope by this Day the money having been sent on to finish the Purchase. Our commercial connections and Plans for Trade & Population being both advantageous & Extensive we trust will within a very

[p. 72[1]]

short time progress our matters to a Degree of respectability & magnitude which must accelerate their Perfection & give them their true dignity. Doctor Fallon can make every Proper communication on the Subject.

Your Polite Offer of being Interested with us will be soon submitted to the Board, & I am certain will meet with due attention which shall be communicated in Time, and your Chearfull tender of Services towards the establishment of our Settlement must afford us in their Operation such Proofs of your zeal & good wishes for the Interest of the company as will ensure no doubt such an Unequivocal Interest to you therein as we hope will be well worthy your Pursuit.

Alexr. Moultrie Director
So. Carola. Yazoo Compy.

Genl. Jno. Sevier

Alex. Moultrie
1790
So. Ca. Yazoo Land Compy.

[p. 73]

S. C. Cha: Ton So. Carolina.

Instructions to James O'Fallon Esquire Principal Agent for the South Carolina Yazoo Company, for the Time being, in the Countries of Kentucky, & the Western Waters the Territory of the said Company and at the City of New Orleans given at Charleston by the Grantees and the rest of the Members of the said Company then present.

1st:

You are to Proceed without delay from Charleston to Lexington in Kentucky. You are there and in the Adjacent Western Territory to investigate the best and most infallible means of procuring a large emigration from thence & the Countries above, to our Territory & to put the same in a train of Action ready for the first Notice, & to communicate the Extent of such means to the Company as Speedily as possible.

2d.

On your arrival at Lexington you are to obtain an Account of such Goods as have been sent there by Col Holder: of what are disposed & for what Purposes & of such as are not yet disposed; to collect if Possible the value of such as have been disposed in mode most adapted to the Purport of this Mission, & to have the remainder, with what now goes by Captn. Cape consolidate one Stock for Satisfying the Choctaw Indians for any Claim may be yet remaining for their Grant & as Presents to them.

3d.

When your values are thus collected or if there requires dispatch, soon as the Goods arrive by Captn. Cape You are with them & such Funds as you can collect to Prepare for a negociation with the Choctaws to which Purpose you are to send a Proper Person as courier to that Nation, & have a meeting. You are then in best manner

Possible to satisfy their Demands, & fix & ... close the Negociation of the grant & the Settlement of Territory & form the firmest Alliance with us possible a ... and defensive Allies; & in which every due regard is had, to giving them a full Conviction, of the Utility to them such a Measure, & to impress it strongly on their Minds. If you shou'd find it Necessary to have an immediate inter

[p. 73[1]]

with the Indians before Captn. Cape arrives, let the Goods Col. Holder will furnish be applied for that Purpose & let them know those are a Coming, of which also immediate Notice must be given to the Company.

4th

A Subagent is to be appointed for Kentucky & the western Country above & such other Place as you think proper, & one for the Companies ...ory: After the measures are fixed in the next preceding article the Companies Agent in Kentucky will be preparing for moving with Emigrants & be ready on the Shortest notice from the Company to send down such a Body & on such terms as they shall direct. a Body of three or four hundred more or Less will in mean Time (if prudent ... do it Peaceably) move down with you. Mr. Woods & such ... you shall choose as most proper to pursue & Address to Assist in Conducting the Business & begin their Settlement in conjunction with same & as many of the confidential Indians as will be a Sanction & ... Agent for the District the Territory remain to move with the main Body after ...able Possession is established.

5th

on your Arrival at Yazoo Spring the first small Party, you will Proceed to Orleans, & under the sanction of your Credentials take such Communications to those in Power there as will convince them of the advantages which will arise to them ... the Spanish Settlements from our vicinity: & that we wish them fully to conceive with us that our views & Interests ... be mutual & reciprocally Friendly: that we esteem ... object of Importance to us both & highly worthy of a last... Cultivation. You are then also to secure the Spanish ...st in our Settlement, as the first Political Bond of attachment to them.

6th

... Kentucky Yazoo, & New Orleans you are to cause ...pentuck information to be transmitted the Company,

[p. 73[2]]

shewing the date & Progress of every measure & incident & you are to Cause a constant Chain of Correspondence to be kept up by You through each Department to the Company & to forward such Confidential Intelligence as may be necessary from time to Time.

7th

Your measures are to be disclosed to such of the Agents of any the Departments as your own Prudence shall direct to you, & you are to repose your confidence when you think best & to the Extent you may deem safest, for the good of the Company.

8th

The Agent of Kentucky & the Country above are to be within your countroul, & where agencies are requisite you are to appoint under you with such extent of Power within your own as may be needfull & so as to Effect the objects of your Commission.

9th

You are to ... the Nation of the Choctaws the strongest ... Agriculture ... Educate ... their children ... promise ...

10th

In all things you are to study Peace ... at as much ... all ... and ... the ... of Justice & accomodation ... & establish the settlement ... most Peaceable & firmest Footing.

11th

By the Na... all Agents in the Service of the Company ... be ... to you ... General Wilkinson & Col: Holder will no doubt be of Service ... in their respective Departments when you ... new Appointments will be made: the ... Departments of ... of Yazoo Shou'd be filled immed...

12th

You are to ... made with the Choctaws ... a Licence & a good Character from the Director ... to request the Indians to say ... Saving ... to Licence to Trade with them that Travels & Injuries may be presented.

[p. 73[3]]

13th:

You are to keep an Agent also amongst the Choctaws on whose Influence & good Character you can rely.

14th

You are to take Care & every Efficient means to prevent People sett... down on the Territory before the Company fixes the Mode of Settlement: excepting the few that may move down before that Period, according to your own Prudential Management & Judgment.

15th:

Above all Things let the Attatchment of the Spaniards and the Choctaws be the Object & make it their Interest. The Goods Col. Holder has & those to be sent by Capt. Cape will I think do the Business:

Axr. Moultrie
Director So. Car:
Yazoo Comp.
9th March 1790

INDEXING NOTE

Page numbers used as locators in the index refer to those stamped or handwritten on the pages of the original manuscript, which appear in the microfilmed edition of the manuscript of Volume 1V. These numbers also correspond to the page numbers appearing in brackets in the transcript.

Every occurrence of all personal names appearing in Volume 1V is indexed, using last, first, and middle names when available. When only a last name is used in the manuscript, the first name is supplied in brackets when it can be determined with reasonable certainty from other sources. Titles such as military rank, academic degree, or political office are used with personal names only if no given name is provided in the manuscript. If neither given name nor title is available, the person is indexed as e.g. Mr. or Mrs. at the surname.

The original spellings of personal and place names are preserved in the transcription. Such spellings frequently vary. In the index, spellings of these names are normalized to the most commonly occurring variants of the full names, with alternate spellings being given in parentheses at the main heading for the name. Other variant spellings of names, if these appear elsewhere in the alphabetically arranged index, are cross-referred to the main heading for the name. (Double posting is used for variant spellings of infrequently occurring names.) Surnames beginning with "Mc" are arranged in the index as if beginning with "Mac", and those beginning with "St." as if beginning with "Saint". Word-by-word sorting has been employed in ordering the index headings.

INDEX

A

B

C

G

H

I

J

K

L

N

O

P

Q

R

U

V

W

Y

Z

Other books by the author:

South Carolina Papers, Volume 1TT of the Draper Manuscript Collection

The George M. Bedinger Papers in the Draper Manuscript Collection

The Illinois Manuscripts, Volume 1Z of the Draper Manuscript Collection

The Mecklenburg Declaration

The Virginia Papers, Volume 1, Volume 1ZZ of the Draper Manuscript Collection

The Virginia Papers, Volume 2, Volume 2ZZ of the Draper Manuscript Collection

The Virginia Papers, Volume 3, Volume 3ZZ of the Draper Manuscript Collection

The Virginia Papers, Volume 4, Volume 4ZZ of the Draper Manuscript Collection

The Virginia Papers, Volume 5, Volume 5ZZ of the Draper Manuscript Collection

Made in the USA
Middletown, DE
07 June 2023

32232352R00161